God's Blueprint for Nations

The KNIGHTS are Rising to SAVE AMERICA and the NATIONS OF THE World

By Don W. Long

ISBN: 978-1-7364162-1-1

Free Gift

As a way of saying "Thank You" to my readers, I have a special gift for you. Click on the link below to access the free Blueprint Training.

www.DonWLong.com/Free-Training

Table of Contents

Introduction

There's a Trumpet blowing right now, an alarm if you will, calling out to all who can hear. This sound is inviting us to become a catalyst in our attempt to save this nation. The epic battle for western civilization is at hand! The remnant is rising for such a time as this. The Father is unleashing a wave of reformers and He's calling us to step in now to restore and rescue our nation. There is an unusual and intense group of people that He is calling for this time; like a wrecking ball, they are arriving in every sphere of influence with His glory upon them and His zeal burning in their hearts. The Lord began to uncover this revelation and insights to me, of what this group would look like as they burst forth onto the stage of history. In Joel 2:7-11, we see a glimpse of what they will be like and what their role shall be:

"They shall run like mighty men; they shall climb the wall like men of war; and they shall march everyone on his ways, and they shall not break their ranks:

Neither shall one thrust another; they shall walk everyone in his path: and when they fall upon the sword, they shall not be wounded.

They shall run to and fro in the city; they shall run upon the wall; they shall climb up upon the houses; they shall enter in at the windows like a thief.

The earthquakes before them, the heavens tremble: the sun and the moon shall be dark, and the stars shall withdraw their shining:

The Lord gives voice before His army, for His camp is very great; for strong is the one who executes His word. For the day of Lord is great and very terrible who can endure it?"

This group will stand strong to execute His word and will, in this season of great uncertainty of our nation's path forward, step in, and be history makers and cultural agents of change. They will not bow before the current politically correct crowd nor give place to the religious spirit that has blinded and silenced the church. In our absence of engagement at the governing gates of all the spheres of influence, we have surrendered our society's high places to the darkness that has almost destroyed our nation. What darkness? All thoughts, ideas, or concepts that malign the very founding that placed our great nation on His eternal Word with His hand guiding and leading us in our birth. The thoughts and actions that we've allowed to rule in the gates of our cities will ultimately lead us to the destruction of the great American experiment if we don't turn back to our **Eternal roots NOW!**

One Worldview

We're in a time and a season when we must stand up and have something of substance to say. If we don't step into the fray now, when will we?

Will it be acceptable in America to say there is no God? Is it going to be acceptable in America there is no law, only the one we create in our image? Are we going to be okay with the spirit of relativism? It is alive and well and only embraces what's relative now, regardless of the future impact. It doesn't consider any absolutes of the past that have brought our nation to its greatness. The worldview of this kind of thought is based on temporal values, not the eternal foundation from which our nation was birthed. Will we black out all the absolutes in our society and allow this spirit of darkness and ungodliness to put us in slavery more than we already are?

Is it okay to teach our children at six, seven, or eight years old that they might be a woman caught in a man's body or a man caught in a woman's body? Can we allow those in our school systems to determine and propagate this as an option? Will that be okay? It's happening in our school systems NOW!

Is it okay that most movies and shows produced in Hollywood project that sin is the lifestyle to live because it elicits pleasure? Is it okay that all the damnation and ungodliness coming out of the movies is more graphic than anything we've seen before? I cannot find one movie on the movie channel that would be acceptable for my wife and me to watch.

I'm not a prude, and I enjoy watching some action movies with graphic scenes in them, like *Braveheart* and *Gladiator*. However, I'm noticing a bend towards purposely making ungodly, dark, and trashy shows so that viewers become desensitized to the violence, sexual perversion, and the attack on anything Godly. What if this graphic violence is the tipping point for those who are already mentally unstable, sending them over the edge, and they go out and shoot and kill 15 or 20 people? We blame guns when this happens. Perhaps we should blame the ungodly brainwashing currently being produced in our entertainment industry.

It's becoming easier to settle for the trash the industry keeps producing, and we watch more of the things that we would have rolled our eyes at just twenty years ago. We feed ourselves on this trash and wonder why so much ungodliness and disruption of absolutes exists in our nation. We need a group of believers to invade Hollywood and champion shows from the heart of the Father that are creative, full of life, and excellent at delivering relative content for the world today. If we continue to let the world create all of what we watch, we will continue getting what we have now. I want to go on record at this point and say that I am not for imposing some moral standard or code of living on other Americans who view the world differently from me. I will defend their right to practice and live what they believe with my life.

Anything you do in the privacy of your home that doesn't harm another is between you and God. This is the way our Founding Fathers viewed our freedom from the Creator in this country, and I do as well. However, I am against people coming outside of their homes, propagating their beliefs, and forcing their worldview on others. Many of those opinions are in direct conflict with my family's faith and values – this is not okay. When I stand up for what I believe and say something about it that is in disagreement with another's worldview, then somehow I am considered to be "not enlightened," "old fashioned," or even worse, a "hater," and there is a desire to cancel my right to free speech. Why am I labeled as anything other than an American when I express what I believe in our country?

For far too long, the church has backed away from being the cultural change agent and walking in its primary call to engage and disciple the nations. We have been absent so long that when we finally attempt to stand up and say something, the cancel culture and political correctness crowd we let fill the void in our absence from the national debate rises and crushes us. We find ourselves in a hostile environment in our nation that was founded on the very faith that now has been marginalized. The moral decay that surrounds us, at the hands of those who would attempt to destroy the very nation we love, has brought us to a very dangerous destination, a place of no return if we don't stand up now!

A rewriting of our great American experiment has been underway for a hundred years! It has been well-crafted by people under the influence of a globalist one worldview. It places your individual freedoms at the mercy of a ruling class with a one worldview, where America is just another cog in the wheel of their one-world system; I believe it has placed us on the **Titanic towards socialism** and a world order which will lead us to the brink of a great unraveling of our life, liberty, and the pursuit of happiness. These unalienable rights that the Creator provided for us are in place because of the sacrifices made by past generations. We are in danger of losing these gifts of freedom in our generation. Let's look at Germany's history to give us an example of how a spirit of darkness can come over an entire nation.

When Hitler took control of Germany, he was a charismatic leader who stepped onto the world stage at a time of great crisis in Germany's history. He promised economic change as they were in a significant downturn and depression from World War I. He promised citizens abundance and new national prominence. They didn't realize they would have to sell their souls to the devil to have that, but that's what happened. It is said that most German people didn't know what was happening to the Jews, which is still debated to this day. Maybe they didn't care as long as their particular ethnic group was okay. Does that sound familiar today? Is this why believers have been silent today – because our lives are so good? Has our prosperity and good life become so dear that we would rather be slaves to the system instead of invading and changing our current culture?

When Hitler rose to power, he removed any voice contrary to his so he could start to systematically remove anything in opposition to him and reeducate the populous in his image for Germany. He began to burn all the books and to rewrite history. Why? Because he only wanted one voice, **His.**

Our Founding Fathers

The books are burning in America right now. The voice of the one worldview and antichrist spirit has risen to be the predominant agenda of those who would attempt to overthrow our nation and freedoms. The foundation of our great nation is being maligned with the Founding Fathers and their faith in God. Their great life sacrifices gave birth to our nation. As the ruling elite class attempts to take away the freedoms others fought and many died for, my question becomes, "Where are the new Founding Fathers and Mothers who will give whatever necessary to take our nation back from the grips of darkness and its well-crafted plan to destroy the greatest and freest nation on earth?" You might ask, "Who is it I'm referring to as 'the ruling elite class.'" This question requires more than a simple one-line answer and could be a book of its own. So, I will give you a couple of quotes from Ben Shapiro's book "The Right Side of History" and recommend you pick a copy up to understand the subject. I believe the following describes who we are at our best and what the ruling class seeks to destroy and remove from our national psyche.

"We believe freedom is built upon the notion that God created every human in His image, and these thoughts were born in Jerusalem and Athens."

"If you believe that government has no right to intrude upon the exercise of your individual will, and that you are bound by moral duty to pursue virtue, you are a product of Jerusalem and Athens. The twin ideals of Judeo-Christian values and Greek natural law of reasoning built human rights. They built prosperity, peace, and artistic beauty. These built America, ended slavery defeated the Nazis and Communist, lifted billons from poverty and gave billons spiritual purpose. Jerusalem and Athens were the foundations of the Magna Carta and the Treaty of Westphalia; they were the foundations of the Declaration of Independence, Abraham Lincoln's Emancipation, and Martin Luther King Jr.'s Letter from Birmingham jail."

The quotes above are indeed where our nation's enemies have attempted to derail us from and have made inroads into our national psyche. We must fight and restore these national foundations and values if we are to save America. Will we do it?

Our founders gave up a lot for our freedom. Out of the 56 people who signed the Declaration of Independence:

- five were captured and tortured before they died
- twelve had their homes burned, two lost their sons in the war
- two had their sons captured
- nine fought and died from either their wounds or the hardships that came out of the Revolutionary War – the war for your freedom here in our great nation.

The moment they signed that document, they became wanted men with a death sentence. If caught, they were hanged immediately or shot. When Hitler took over Germany, the same thing happened. All the people who were already against him were pulled out in the street and eliminated. He got away with it, and society developed a hardness toward killing people. We have in America too, haven't we?

What about babies? How many millions of unborn babies will we kill before we know it's wrong? Will we allow it to be federalized and forced upon people as an option to kill an innocent child after it's born? How long will we keep going in debt to other countries while we're bankrupt in America? How long will we strap trillions of dollars of debt upon the next generation to deal with until we completely collapse the economy through moral decay and financial bankruptcy?

We're there now. We're not *going to be* there; we *are* there already. I'm not a pessimist. I believe that we can save America, but I'm telling you that NOW is the time to step in. If we don't step in now, then when? Will it be when we've lost all of our freedoms? Then will you act? After you've been persecuted and face imprisonment and possibly death? They are burning our books now, and with a well-crafted and executed plan to overthrow our nation after a hundred years, they find themselves almost in charge. The only thing keeping the spirit of darkness through men from ruling the world is America and our faith in our Divine destiny. They are attempting to take all the theology of righteousness and our founding as one nation under God and make us subservient as a people to serve a progressive, imperialist one world-view, with the ruling elite class deciding what's right and which freedoms and choices people should have.

Socialism and Marxism

We are in a war right now for our nation's soul and the freedoms afforded to us by the sacrifice of previous generations. The globalists are attempting to remove everything you take for granted as an American. Your freedoms and the future of your generations are in the balance right now, and if we don't stand up now, we could lose our precious nation. The dangers of this worldview have their foundation in Socialism and Marxism. Every nation that has attempted the Robinhood scheme (taking from one group and giving it to another) has failed. This has never worked and will destroy America if we allow it to be implemented here (look at Venezuela). There's always a progressive individual or group who comes up with new words and plans for selling this utopia to the masses. But just as Margaret Thatcher said, "We have already tried what you're advocating, and it has always failed miserably. Grow up, get a real job for a change, and learn something about history and economics." I believe the biggest threat to our National independence is this very thought process propagated by elites who want to divide and destroy America.

Why do we allow those influenced by darkness and a worldview that will collapse and undermine our nation to run our universities and school systems? Why is it that we allow politics and economics to be controlled by darkness through people when people who have righteous intent could influence them? Why is the entertainment industry primarily controlled by darkness when it should be influenced by light? Why have we as believers in Christ drifted so far away from our Godly founding that there's barely a difference between the world and us? Where is the church's voice concerning the ills of our day that affect us nationally and locally? Many church leaders keep avoiding the hard topics that we as people are facing and struggling with as a Nation. We must begin to preach the whole council of the Word of God and what it looks like to be Leaders and Champions in our individual spheres and national reformers in our country. If we don't, we will continue to suffer under the rule of the unrighteous standard that we have allowed to be built as an altar over us in our nation.

Speak Up

Where can we step in and have a voice in media that is of promise instead of propaganda? Tell me, when will we rise up, having something to say worth listening to and providing answers to the world around us? When will we stop the madness in our country's political atmosphere and replace the people who are doing the wrong things now at the State and Federal levels?

When will it be okay to stand up and say that something is wrong without others considering it hate? I think we're there. We need to step in with an agenda from Heaven that has an edge to it and change this or lose what freedoms we have left.

As Patrick Henry said in his speech before national leaders who were not convinced that it was time to take action yet, *"It is in vain, sir, to extenuate the matter. Gentlemen may cry, "Peace, Peace," but there is no peace. The war has actually begun. The next gale that sweeps from the north will bring to our ears the clash of resounding arms. Our brethren are already in the field. Why stand we here idle? What is it that gentlemen wish? What would they have? Is life so dear, or peace so sweet, as to be purchased at the price of chains and slavery? Forbid it, Almighty God. I don't know what course others may take; but as for me, give me liberty or give me death!"*

My question is, what course are you going to take? Notice Henry said, *"We are saying peace and safety when war is already begun."*

You can say peace all you want. The Word of God in 1 Thessalonians 5:1-3 warned against doing that. We think it's the world saying it when in fact, the church is saying it. We're saying peace, peace, and let's just keep enjoying our party on the Titanic as we head towards the iceberg of destruction. Our confusion grows because of the Powerless Gospel we've embraced that never steps into the arena of National debate with answers from the Father to change our nation's systems from the top down! Where are the Leaders of the church? Where are the righteous voices crying out against the cesspool of darkness controlling and invading our institutions?

I have the same question that was asked to the character of William Wallace in the movie *Braveheart*. He goes through his speech as the armies take up positions on both sides of the battlefield. He ends his speech asking, "Will they fight for their freedom?" Then he says, "Will you give all the moments of your life from now to then to just once tell the enemies, you might take my life, but you will never take my freedom." That's really the question. If we don't stand up now, we are going to be inducted into more slavery. For how long? We don't know. The induction has already started, you just don't realize it. I believe that the Father is pouring out His Spirit to right the wrongs for us to step into the fray and stand up now. If the next great awakening doesn't send us into the tops of our nation's mind molders to lead them, then we will lose our nation as we drift away on the revival boat to neverland.

Will you be one of those who do, or will you be the timid soul who won't go into the arena? True, we may die, we might fail, but my question is, will we dare greatly and step into risk at this moment to save our nation? The choice is yours. The possibilities are endless. The tragedy of our country's destruction is possible as well. We have to change! The time is NOW or there might not be another NOW.

Chapter 1

Bending the Twig

*"The Roots of the Lost Eternal
Foundation of our Nation"*

Just a few short decades ago, our citizens overwhelmingly embraced the values of a Judeo-Christian nation. Upon that foundation, our nation has prospered and grown for well over 200 years. This was the America of my youth, but unfortunately, through a well-crafted plan to overthrow our nation, there has been a relentless attack upon the things that made us the greatest nation on earth. Will we gain a new national sense of our God-given destiny again or be morphed into a new world order under a globalist elite ruling class? We are at a crossroads in our path as a people; what will we choose?

A nation that expects to last and have the blessing of God on it must be founded on something that has His eternal perspective, one that governs with justice and righteousness for all its people. As Benjamin Franklin, one of the Founding Fathers, put it, "I have lived, sir a long time; and the longer I live, the more convincing proofs I see of this truth: that God governs in the affairs of men. And if a sparrow cannot fall to the ground without His notice, is it probable that an empire can rise without His aid?"

The Constitution and the Declaration of Independence are replete with references to the Creator and acknowledge His hand and guidance in establishing our nation. In the last fifty years, the spirit of darkness has crafted a well-organized attack through men on the belief that we should govern from His Words in all the affairs. The attempt to remove the sacred writings and His signature upon our nation has been systemic and unrelenting. The foundation of our government must govern from His eternal laws, with His hand guiding our country as He did in our infancy.

Edmund Burke, a 1700s philosopher and Founding Father, stated, "But what is liberty without wisdom and without virtue? It is the greatest of all possible evils; for it is folly, vice, and madness, without tuition or restraint." Notice that freedom without virtue and wisdom is the greatest of all evils. Without the eternal truth that shaped us, we will fall, and without His wisdom leading us, we will wander in darkness. We must have a government with righteous laws, and righteousness can't be what this or the next generation thinks is hip or cool. It can't be built on relativism, and that truth is only relevant based on the way we see it today and how we feel about it today. It has to be on an Eternal foundation of absolutes.

A display of Commandments 6 through 10 of the Ten Commandments is located in the United States Supreme Court south frieze. These five are typically viewed as the more secular commandments by which a nation would govern. Moses can be seen holding the tablets on which God's law was given to him. Interestingly, they are written in Hebrew text instead of Roman text, which is typically used. Our nation's beginning was placed on the foundation of the Judeo-Christian faith by our Founding Fathers. They realized we needed absolutes to govern by and put their trust in God and the principles of the scriptures of the Bible as their basis and guide. The 10 Commandments are universal in the sense of a governing structure. Having laws based on eternal foundations that don't change creates a solid foundation on which every generation can govern. These eternal standards have been passed down in our nation to protect its entire people.

The laws that govern the United States must be founded on absolutes that don't change. If you read the Declaration of Independence and the Constitution, you'll see the Creator's DNA throughout both because the Founding Fathers wanted it to be the foundation of the country, which it has been. However, it's been under relentless attack for the last 50 to 100 years in a calculated manner. This plan and indoctrination of our nation have brought us to a dangerous tipping point. Will America be the light set on a hill and a nation of people who believe in our birth as inspired and conceived by God Himself? Or will we find ourselves being ruled by a progressive elite who doesn't care about or believe in our God, and would place our freedoms and our nation's life at the tree of the knowledge of good and evil? This represents man's wisdom of governing without God because he (man) supposedly knows best. Let's now explore how you can systematically change the cultural inheritance of a nation within one generation and why I believe that those who would take our nation down the wrong path have prevailed.

In Proverbs, the Word of God says, *"Train a child in the way that they should go, and when they're old, they won't depart from it."* The word "train" can be translated several ways. One meaning is "to bend," and the inference is two-fold. **First,** the child comes with natural gifts and talents, and we as parents should never try and bend them against what the Creator placed in them. **Second,** which is what we are getting at here, through creating an ecosystem in every area of their lives, they can be bent, over time, into whatever mold society dictates.

So, to bend the twig, you are bending the whole tree, if you will, while it's young. The tree will grow in the direction in which it's bent. Children come with a bend inside of them for certain things they will do on Earth as part of their make-up from the Father. But in reality, it is up to the parents, the teachers, rabbis, pastors, and leaders to speak into this child's life to ensure the ecosystem around them is in alignment with Kingdom values. Bending the twig helps create strongholds of righteousness and allows that twig to be built upon the foundations of absolutes: integrity, honesty, discretion, instructions, wisdom, insight, and prudence.

These words help us describe and picture what it looks like to live out Kingdom values in our daily lives. These are not just worldly terms; they're Biblical and based in the book of wisdom, Proverbs. I want you to understand the magnitude of this; whoever disciples the nation from the top down gains the access that causes the bending of every twig in our country, whether they are good or evil. When you start bending the twig from a young age, you produce the next heirs of the nation – the next leaders of everything from Hollywood, media, politics, economics, family, church, and technology. You are building the leaders for that next generation because they have different callings and giftings. Let's look at how this works in a positive environment.

Raising Children in Positive Environments

Through an ecosystem established on eternal values, parents and society bend the twig by placing certain expectations on a child. Teachers bend it the same way, and when the child gets to college, it's bent the same way. As the child grows into an adult and starts discovering their place of destiny in this world, these foundations of eternity have been set in their hearts. Then, all of society supports this same ecosystem that began during youth. Because society is built upon absolutes and something that you can put your feet on as a foundation, over time, our nation's ecosystem is built and put in place on purpose. It is represented through the daily lived-out culture of the people who grow up here. That's the way God intended us to grow this nation, and we did for a long time.

Being bent from a young age in God's ways and His ecosystem enables governing from absolutes in a country to filter down to our children. The alternate to truth is built the same way by bending the twigs with thoughts that truth is relative, and there are no absolutes. This leads us to think there are multiple paths to truth, and it's all relative; and in those Shades of Grey, we begin to define truths based on what's temporal, not that which is eternal. In the movie *Star Wars*, when Obi-Wan Kenobi went on to the afterlife and appeared in a vision to Luke, Luke asks, "Why did you tell me that Darth Vader killed my father?" Notice what Obi-Wan Kenobi says, "In a sense, that is a version of what happened because the good man your father was, Anakin Skywalker, was destroyed by Darth Vader." In essence, it's a version of the truth.

Truth doesn't have versions! Yet, this is what we've done by burning the books, if you will, of the souls of our country through revisionist teaching and rewriting the books that teach our children about our nation's greatness. We have removed the Creator's ideas and heart from the marketplace, education at every level, the political realm, and economics. The self-appointed propaganda programmers, the media and Hollywood, have done really well in their attempts to rewrite our history. They ignore the Founding Father's faith, which caused them to risk everything to birth the greatest nation ever formed on earth that provides freedom and prosperity for all.

In the west, the light, which should be the church, has, in essence, backed away and surrendered all spheres of influence in the last one hundred years. The decay in every nation starts when the church, which should be the nation's moral compass, begins to either pull out of societal places of influences that shape culture or worse, we become part of the problem by endorsing that which the Word of God doesn't. Then, the church becomes part of the decay. The church should be the truth meter of a nation; the just standard of a nation; the preachers of righteousness. When those preachers of righteousness start limiting what they'll say because of a personal offense or straddle the fence based on what the politically correct crowd thinks, we become more interested in what's popular or hip and cool than Truth. Then, our light is darkened, and we begin to create the wrong standard.

We are now raising the next generation of those who will run our high schools and colleges, and our businesses and political system.

They'll be leading our churches and the arts, entertainment, and media in Hollywood. Now, we're bending the twig with mixed shades of grey. As a nation, are we worse or better off morally than we were fifty years ago? Are we worse or better off in the area of indebtedness? Are we worse or better off in marriage statistics? Are we worse or better off in the movies we put out and what they endorse? Do they propagate righteousness or unrighteousness? Are we better or worse off in our education systems? Is media more positive than it was 50 years ago? Or would you consider it more bent towards agenda-ism instead of reporting the news and telling the Truth?

You make the call. I think you already know the answer. If you've bent the million-plus twigs in America over a generation, then suddenly, right is wrong, and wrong is right. The great communist leader Lenin says, "A lie told long enough becomes the truth." Bending and twisting our great nation's ecosystem has been happening for the last 50 to 100 years. Now, many of these twigs are full-grown trees that are bent the wrong way, and they're running everything.

This all started with the church's disengagement from the places of influence due to what I believe is a flawed theology. We taught people to either be separated from the world or not be involved in shaping the culture. In doing so, we have taken light out and allowed darkness to come in and exert its influence over our nation. When the church won't step in and bring the answers that our country needs from the Creator's heart, then our whole society will look for the answers from other places. The only issue is we have only two choices: we can get answers from light or darkness. There's no multiple choice in this arena. If you bend the twig the wrong way, you create a mechanism that develops in a child, producing strongholds towards whatever the bend is. Eventually, a stronghold becomes an anchored, automatic behavior that exists even if the original information or thoughts that started to change you are no longer there. The instructions don't need to be present; it becomes automatic. It's a mechanism of brainwashing your mind and bending you. The stronghold becomes the thing that runs your life, whether it's a stronghold of righteousness or unrighteousness.

These lives become communities, then cities, then a bunch of cities. They create a state's ecosystem. Then, all states become an ecosystem that governs our nation, whether it's built-on righteousness or unrighteousness. That's how it's built, and it only takes one generation. We're one generation away from being slaves. Likewise, we are one generation away from a new level of freedom. This is what our Founding Fathers believed. In many areas, we've already been made slaves by losing freedoms for which our Founding Fathers fought and died. The Creator is raising visionaries and pioneers to bend the twigs the other way. This will take time, possibly 25 to 50 years, but I believe we must start at once. It won't happen overnight. We must be in it for the long haul and be foundationally sound in this attempt to save our nation based on the Creator's standard of absolutes. If we're not going to do it now, my question is, when will we do it? Just think about that. Is it not bad enough yet?

"All it takes for evil to triumph is for good men and women to do nothing," said Edmund Burke. This seems too big to save America from her current plight. That's what I said, too. The Father said this through Edmund Burke 250 years ago. "He that does nothing because he can only do little has made no greater mistake." My question to you is, what can you do to change the bend of the youth in our country and our society? What can you do to bend the twig back to the moral foundation of absolutes, which are Kingdom values? What is it that you can do? What's in your hands that you need to do and do with all your heart and all your strength now? If you don't do it now, when would you do it? Is it going to be now or sometime in the future? And the future never comes. Will you die with the music in you, or will you give everything you have to save your country, children, and your children's children? Are you going to step in the fray and do what you can to bend our national psyche back to Kingdom values?

Let now be now, and let's move at once. We can start this journey to hand off to our children to keep it going. Let's bend our national psyche back to that which the Founding Fathers saw as the future of a great nation, that it would be established upon moral absolutes. The reality is that our Founding Fathers wanted people to be free at all costs. But freedom is not for slaves because slaves don't know how to live in freedom. As Edmund Burke says, "Liberty is not for people without virtue or wisdom. If they don't have virtue and wisdom, it is the worst of all possible evils." Freedom becomes the worst of all possible evils if you don't have virtue or wisdom. Virtue is truth. Absolutes. Wisdom is God's thoughts on how to govern a nation and how to govern yourself. Self-government. Freedom isn't created for people who don't know how to govern themselves. This is the amble, the marking of our Constitution and the Declaration of Independence of our great nation. It's self-government and intended to be governed from a place of virtue and wisdom so that you can live in freedom. But liberty is the most possible evil when it doesn't have virtue and wisdom, restraint and discretion.

So, the question becomes, where do we start, and is there precedent in the scriptures to build on? We see in Luke 16:8 that Jesus said, *"The sons of darkness are wiser in their generation than the sons of light,"* meaning they're smarter than us. As I was writing a book with a business context, I asked the Lord, "What do the sons of darkness do when they fail?" He said, "They don't use me as their scapegoat." Wow! That slapped me on the head. He continued, "They market harder, do different things, ask better questions, ask, 'Why did I fail?' They look at their execution or staff that's in place. Do we have the right people? Are we getting to our best clients? Do we need better implementation or strategies? They ask the questions that any good businessperson should be asking. And instead of blaming God, they pivot and go after it again." We see another passage of scripture in which Jesus says, *"Be wise as serpents. But harmless as doves."* (Matthew 10:16). We have the harmless part down, but we don't have a clue how to use the wisdom that God is talking about here to implement change that He desires into our world. There's a wisdom in being wise as a serpent, and I believe a shrewdness in how we are to operate similarly to the sons of darkness according to the Master's teachings Himself. When we go into the world systems around us, outwardly, we are to be wise as serpents, full of shrewd wisdom and the power of sagacity, but inwardly, our true identity as the dove or the very presence of the Holy Spirit whom we carry into the world.

These two passages of scripture give us the paradigm shift we need to be effective in the world. We must acknowledge these passages because this is Jesus Himself teaching us how to operate in the world. We must understand what it's like to be in the world with answers coming from Him, delivered through wisdom and shrewdness, but not be of the world. So, as we explore how to extend the Kingdom of God through being wise as serpents and also having influence like the sons of darkness as Jesus himself taught, I want you to understand that the wisdom and influence that He is talking about in those scriptures are from the Father.

I know that the first time He dealt with me about this subject. My first objection to writing this book was people won't want to be compared to the serpent, but that's not what He said. As I studied and received more revelation, I realized that He wanted us to use the very wisdom He placed in the serpent and the insights that the unjust steward used in which he was commended by the Master Himself in Luke 16-8. Both are His protype for invading and influencing culture. He's not saying to become like them but be as wise as the world when implementing His ways in building the Kingdom of God. He really is a Genius; we just need to follow His instructions. He began to unpack how to move in influence and favor in the world, and I was amazed at how He spelled out His wisdom and insights in the scriptures like a blueprint. If we follow His instructions, success will come. Let's jump into some of those insights and wisdom.

The Kingdom of God

The world propagates its ideas using the systems and structures the Creator put in place for their benefit. Through the mindset of seedtime and harvest, they continually sow ideas that get inside the culture without you knowing they are there (a little leaven leavens the whole lump.) This is how the Kingdom of God works, and I believe innately the world has picked up on it, at somewhat of a subconscious level, and uses it to their benefit. In Matthew 13:24-33, we have three examples of how the Kingdom of God works and is implemented. **First,** we see that the enemy sowed tares among the wheat as the men slept. **Second**, we see that the mustard seed is the smallest seed, but once it's planted, it becomes the largest tree of the herb family. **Finally**, when leaven is put in dough, it leavens the whole thing.

Let's look at these three examples and find common ground in each story. Notice that the Kingdom comes in covered from plain sight, the seeds are the smallest among the trees but become the largest, and the leaven of the Kingdom can change the composition of anything in which it is placed. So, here's what that might look like. Instead of tares, we plant wheat. When? At night when no one is watching. The seed is planted in the darkness of the soil. The leaven is inside the lump working where no one can see it until it leavens the whole thing. I believe this is how we should operate, and it is definitely how the world works, "*precept upon precept, upon precept, line upon line and line upon line here a little and there a little*." (Isaiah 28:13) Suddenly, as the lump realizes it's been leavened, it's too late. We can see that Jesus is giving us the keys to build the Kingdom in these scriptures, but for whatever reason, we haven't taught these subjects in a practical sense, so their implementation can change culture. The very truths contained in these references have been turned on us and used against us by the enemy. He has attempted to create his narrative for what we think is possible in this life.

This takes us to the point where our beliefs become eroded and change little by little over time. Your beliefs can be systematically redesigned by the ecosystem built in the culture of your country, state, city, and your home, and you don't know it's happening. It's like the frog being boiled. This is what has happened to our nation. You can see that the people in the world who might or might not know the Creator used the way He set the earth up to grow and produce what's been planted. Through their systematic effort, they have gained control of the high places and gates of our nation.

The cunningness and wisdom of the serpent moves in covertly. It observes and pays attention to what's going on, and then slips its little thoughts in bit by bit, where they're not abrasive, like little darts. Do you remember that the shield of faith is for the fiery darts? The fiery darts of the enemy come in little thoughts. Over time, your beliefs erode, and you begin to anchor in your heart at the cellular level, the new thoughts that start as small darts. We see in Proverbs 4:23, *"Keep your heart with all vigilance, for from it flows the springs of life."* In this scripture, the statement 'flows the spring of life' is interesting because it means that the spring can be filled with death or life since you choose what's allowed into your heart. Paul, in Colossians 3:2 states, *"Set your affections on things above, not on things on the earth"* or earthly mindsets that don't line up with His thoughts and ways. Why? Whatever you feed on with your affections will be reproduced in your heart. The heart is neutral based on what you feed it or allow to be sowed into it, even if it's done without you being conscious of it. Why? Because whatever proceeds out of your heart is what your life will produce, whether it's good or bad.

We were introduced to subliminal advertising through movies in the 1960s. You may remember many movie theatres would play a Coca-Cola commercial before a movie. The message in the ad would contain a hidden message that the conscious mind didn't pick up on, and you would develop a sensation telling you, "I need a Coke." If you gave into that feeling, then you would find yourself at the counter buying a Coke. These ads attached a positive feeling inside you so that whenever you saw it, not only at the movies, you would have the same feeling and find yourself buying another bottle of Coke. This type of advertising became the new norm, attempting to produce an emotion in you similar to that of Pavlov's dogs. The Pavlovian theory was developed as a learning procedure that involves pairing a stimulus with a conditioned response, meaning that the advertisement was the stimulus. The feeling that came was the response. All of the ads were not necessarily built around the subliminal piece, but they were definitely built to engage your feelings so you would respond. Because this type of advertising was so successful, companies realized they could get the same response if their ads got consumers to feel something at a cellular level (all the way through the nervous system). So, this became a new way for companies to introduce the world to the products they were selling.

Here's another example that will allow you to see how powerfully others can use your state of mind and feelings to anchor a belief leading to action. My wife would often stay with her Uncle Tom, who was like her grandfather, and his wife for the weekend. She and Tom would go to the country store or his favorite golf club and have a bottle of Coke and a pack of peanuts. Her love for Uncle Tom and the love and strength he gave back to her in these times left an indelible mark on her feelings and psyche. To this day, when we go somewhere that sells old-fashioned bottles of Coke, she always has one. When she opens it and drinks it, she relives that same feeling of the eight-year-old girl even though it's been over fifty years. That feeling is anchored to something positive in her life, a positive role model.

The same thing can occur in a negative sense. Deception and delusion are sowed into your heart the same way Truth is put in you. The enemy can also use the systemic process the Father designed for your good to produce evil. The enemy can only copy the original that

God created and distort it; he can't create anything new. He uses the same three protypes mentioned in Matthew 13:24-33; he has no new tools, only the ones the Creator initiated in the beginning. We need to move into our individual spheres of influence by being wise as serpents, and then look, observe, and learn how we should go into the place we are called to and plant the seeds of the Kingdom. The enemy came in at night and sowed tares among the wheat under darkness; no one could see them or detect they had been there until it was too late.

We haven't quite understood this principle, but the world understands this because the *"Sons of darkness are wiser in their generation than the sons of light."* (Luke 16:8). I hope our generation will see this as an invitation from the Lord, step into the world, and do something about it. We need to bend the next generation of children towards righteousness and send them as mighty men and women of righteousness into the spheres of our society. They will grow and understand how to slip in unnoticed and start planting and propagating the culture of the Kingdom. Suddenly, you will see that ecosystem rise on that particular mountain, and we'll gain it back. This starts with you and me.

The Truth meter of our nation, the church, has for too long backed away from the gates of influence to stay separate from the world. This has caused the world to slip into politics, education, media, arts, economics, and family and disciple our nation with its ideology. We are at a dangerous point in history that requires us to step in now or suffer the consequences that might be irreversible in our lifetime. Our version of Christianity in the west has become voiceless and complacent in our societal evolution and impact! This must change Now! Many leaders have taught us a lifestyle that causes us to pull away from the world instead of stepping in to do our duty. If you think that I am off in my observation, then compare our Christianity in America today and those who profess to be believers to our Founding Fathers' faith and their view of Christianity and its role in birthing our great nation as well as governing and fighting for our freedom. Their faith caused them to engage at every level of society, while ours has caused a retreat or an indifferent and apathetic attitude. We must step into the battle for our nation's soul or lose the freedoms we gained through the sacrifice of those who have gone before us, whose faith overcame all odds to birth this great nation.

Let me ask you a question. From the standpoint of Christian values and of the Kingdom thought, are we prevailing in any areas of cultural influence in our nation? Are we better now than we were 30 years ago by any metrics? Are our children better off now versus thirty years ago? I grew up in an America where we didn't need to lock our doors. When I was only ten years old, I could ride my bike to school without worry about what might happen to me. I could go on and on about how it was in my childhood, but if you are over 50 years of age, you remember what it was like. We see in Proverbs 9-1 that there's seven pillars that wisdom can build over a nation to mold a nation's psyche, *"Wisdom hath built her house, she has hewn out her seven pillars."* There could be more, but I think the most significant pillars include Government, Economics, Media, Education, Family, Church, Arts, and Entertainment.

The good news is it only takes three to five percent of a population to shift culture and create change to reverse the curse. According to Malcolm Gladwell's book *The Tipping Point*, three things are needed to shift a culture: **the law of the few, the stickiness factor, and the power of context.** As a people, we must go up the spheres of societal influence and gain a voice again through these three things working with us to change the affairs and direction of our nation. The only way to have a reformation and a great awakening that changes our nation is to ascend the systems and gain influence through the answers we bring from the Creator.

Chapter 2

Beliefs

In the last chapter, we talked a little about subliminal advertising and the Pavlovian theory, which was developed as a learning procedure that involves pairing a stimulus with a conditioned response. The Pavlovian theory was used mainly on dogs, but it can be modified to affect people, as we've seen in the advertising piece. I want to talk more about how beliefs are developed and how you can change them once they are set inside you. Over our lifetime, certain things become set inside of us that may not be entirely true. We need to be aware that we develop all of our beliefs over time through many avenues, such as life experiences, mentors, parents, teachers, culture, and society. All of these avenues come through people's insights and the knowledge they currently have. So, some of what's taught can have flaws or is only what they learned to this point, meaning there's possibly more truth they haven't discovered yet. Have you ever received a new insight about something you believed, and then one day, you realized it wasn't really the way you thought?

I'll start with a story of a great-great-grandmother who always cut her ham in half to cook it, and it was the best ham around. All of her kids, grandkids, and great-grandkids would do the same because they like the way hers tasted. Eventually, one of her granddaughters asked her mother, "Why do you cut your ham in half to cook it? I've never seen anyone else do that." The mother replied, "Well, I don't know, but that's the way momma did it." So, she asked her great-grandmother, who replied, "Well, that's easy honey. Our ovens were too small to put the whole piece in there."

Generations of women in that family cut a ham in half to cook it when the oven was big enough to hold the entire ham. Why? Because they believed it was the best way to cook ham because it tasted really good when great-great-grandmother did it like that. Beliefs set in us may make sense to one generation but are not necessarily true for every generation.

Some beliefs that are based on biblical and eternal value are set in stone forever. I'm not talking about those; I'm talking about beliefs that we buy into. I want to talk about how we develop beliefs. Unfortunately, we don't realize that we can believe a lie as easily as we believe the truth. You might think you're above that but understand that truth and lies propagate and grow the same way; they both start in the seed form of thought and words that eventually lead to actions. Taken long enough, those actions turn into strongholds, which are nothing more than automatic actions you begin to take without natural thought. In other words, they become second nature, and you don't question the belief any longer.

Truth is put into people a little at a time like you would sow a seed, grow a crop, or put leaven into a piece of dough. You put a little bit in it, and it leavens a whole lump. If done right, truth is put into people in small increments from the time they're small until they are grown. Hopefully, that society's ecosystem supports putting the particular truth into the person or the child. A lie is implanted the same way. (The Devil can't create anything new; he can only use what's been created.) Little by little, and eventually, your belief system becomes wrapped around that particular truth or that particular lie. We see in Isaiah 28:10, "*For precept must be upon precept, precept upon precept, line upon line and line upon line, here a little and there a little.*" The truth and the lie are built the same way, over time, into a culture until it is second nature, whether it be good or bad.

Our nation is in the greatest moral decline, the greatest bankruptcy of finances and economics, and upon the greatest threshold of entering Dante's Inferno and never returning. Our nation has lost its bearing in so many ways over my lifetime. Based on what I see in most believers I meet, we have either through ignorance or apathy, backed away and left the conversation about impact at the tops of influence in our nation. I believe that the Father will raise a new set of Founding Fathers and Mothers who can turn the tide right now in America. He has people ready. Some are ready right now, but they don't have a catalyst. There is no trumpet blowing or a movement and a cause to get behind, but they feel the same frustrations as you and I.

Light is the only thing that can bring light. That's a profound statement, I know. Darkness cannot bring light, and therefore, the world and the people in the world cannot save America without the hand of God. Only the people who believe in Providence and His way of building nations, and are willing to step in the fray, can save America at this point. It's going to take a move from Heaven to earth to save our country with people who will carry it unashamedly with power and authority and will begin to speak the truth again no matter what it costs.

Beliefs and Truths

Most believers don't understand the correlation between their beliefs and feelings. Your beliefs are only your beliefs because of something that's built in you over time, through repeated thoughts, words, and actions that you consistently embrace. By and large, experiences and encounters form what we believe. When these are anchored into your heart long enough through your emotions and feelings at a cellular level, they are set inside you and become convictions, which is a belief on steroids. In other words, when it's that deep in you, you will die for it. Let me put it to you this way… if you don't feel something at a cellular level, meaning all the way through, then it's not real for you whether it is real in actuality or not.

Unfortunately, most of us don't understand how we're created with our cortex and the lymphatic part of our brain that is rational. But really, our spirit or subconscious mind keeps us alive and runs everything inside of us without natural thought. For instance, you have a fight-or-flight part of you to keep you alive in crisis. It is innate in that it acts outside of natural thought. If you had to think about a lion that is going to kill you, you wouldn't run or get out the way fast enough. You don't think first; you move from a feeling on the inside. That fight-or-flight response inside you is intuitive and makes you move without natural thought. It is subconscious thought which can discern and think at billions of bits of information per second instead of thousands of bits per second with natural thought.

I want you to think about beliefs and truths. This is the way that the Creator made you and is not some crazy science somebody came up with to sell a book. This is actually the way you were created. Your physical body, spirit, and soul are all tied together. Nobody will argue that our subconscious and spirit supersede our mental capacity. That's not up for debate. Many things come into our life at a subconscious or a spiritual level that we don't even think about but just take in and consume. In the book, "Self-Health Revolution" by J. Michael Zenn, Chapter Six, "The Ultimate Brain Doctor," shows us how powerful we are. A few things Zenn mentions:

- Our eyes can take in more than 10 million different color distinctions, taking in more information than the most powerful telescope known to man.

- Our ears can discriminate 1600 hundred frequencies at once.

- Your heart beats 100,000 times a day and pumps blood through 1,000 miles of arteries without you even thinking about it!

Wow! Did you realize you were that powerful?

Neurosciences have discovered many details of how fearfully and wonderfully we are made. Through these discoveries, which began in the early 1970s, we have a context for how beliefs can be encouraged to change over time. I believe that this discovery is, for the most part, in agreement with the way the Creator made us. In layman's terms, a belief is developed by seeing something repeatedly and attaching a certain feeling to it. That feeling becomes habitually anchored inside of you, and that anchor becomes a stronghold you would defend to the death. It becomes a conviction. It gets driven down inside you at the cellular level, where you feel it through your whole body, soul, and spirit. That belief becomes a stronghold of conviction for which people will give their lives. Trust me, the people who blow themselves up with a bomb believe in their cause. They have bought in at a cellular level where everything inside of them is anchored. The thought and feeling has become so strong that it produced a stronghold, and they are willing to die for their cause, whether it's right or wrong.

All beliefs begin with propagating an environment much like you would when planting things in a garden that you want to grow. You create an ecosystem and start developing individual plantings into that culture. As you develop the ecosystem and culture, you begin propagating the particular environment that will cause that plant to grow as you want, producing the perfect environment for the plant's health and longevity. When disciplining a nation, it's called social architecture and engineering. When the people at the top decide what stimulus to introduce in the form of thoughts and the conditioned response, they seek to build the culture into the design they had in mind. Whether it be light or darkness, both propagate and implement seeds of systematic thoughts that gain entry inside your belief system repeatedly until it gets down in you. Your beliefs are groomed over time by attaching either a positive or negative feeling to it. You will adjust what you believe by the feelings attached, whether the emotion is intensely good or bad.

Propaganda and repetitive comments and statements enter your eyes and your ear gate, eventually affecting your heart. Your heart is your spirit, or as some people call it, your subconscious. In layman's terms, you can put a particular belief on TV, the Internet, or printed news and repeat it over and over again, saying it from different angles, and you can change the way people perceive it. Enlisting some positive things about that belief will cause people to have feelings and emotions that feel good to them. The reverse is true as well if negative things are stated about the belief. Either way, the propaganda machine wins by the way it makes you feel. If you are not extremely vigilant, your intense emotions start to override past beliefs because of those feelings and intense images.

Over time, people start buying in little by little, and develop a belief. You can use a counter-propaganda machine to undo beliefs that have been built in society for hundreds of years. Take the weapons that oppose those beliefs and start propagating them, creating an eco-system and causing the individual cultures and plants to grow. People will begin to believe certain things because of the feelings produced from the thought coming in repeatedly. This is how you remove what's right or wrong from a whole generation. The systems the Creator put in place will funnel through them, through the spirit of those who govern the high places, at the gates of social architecture, whether they be the truth or a lie.

Joseph Goebbels provides a glimpse into how an unrighteous eco-system is developed, saying, *"If you tell a lie big enough and keep repeating it, people will eventually come to believe it. The lie can be maintained only for such time as the state can shield the people from the political, economic, and military consequences of the lie."* The above quote is how I believe America has found herself in its current state.

If we are so full of light, why is our country so dark? If you think the church in America is so full of light, then why is it silent? Why is our culture collapsing and our country's foundation crumbling without us saying or doing anything? Well, I can tell you why. The propaganda machine has done its job well. We have been lulled into silence by the antichrist, one-world view that attempts to destroy America and our freedoms that the Creator provided at our founding. Dietrich Bonhoeffer said, *"Silence in the face of evil is itself evil; God will not hold us guiltless. Not to speak is to speak. Not to act is to act."*

The propaganda machine and the counter-propaganda machine work the same way. Jesus gives us three examples of how to enact a cultural ecosystem change. **Number one:** "It only takes a little leaven to leaven a whole lump." **Number two:** He talks about the mustard seed being the smallest seed amongst seeds. But it grows into this large tree where, over time, birds make their homes. **Number three:** There's a field sown with wheat, and at night, an enemy plants tares among the wheat, attempting to destroy it by competing for the root system and the nutrients in the field. He is showing us the way the Kingdom works to produce societal change. These three things give you insight into how beliefs in our nation are either built positively or destroyed negatively. We think we're immune to this, but we're not.

The Word of God shows us when the Pharisees were talking to Jesus about the disciples not washing their hands, He told the Pharisees, "You shouldn't worry about what goes in your mouth and body; that is not what corrupts you. What comes out of your heart is what corrupts you." If you sow seed long enough into your heart through watching and seeing, you will shift and change what you believe over time. You become like the frog in the pan. You're relaxing in the water when it gets a little warmer, and you start sweating. Before you realize what's happening, you're boiled to death by the very thing you were enjoying.

Most of us are unaware and don't realize how beliefs are built or torn down. We are not as rational and logical as we think.

The last step to developing a belief in us is rationalization. Everyone thinks we're logical and rational beings first, but we're not – at least not at the beginning of the thought process. You believe something because of a conditioned response through repeated stimuli given to you. It gets into your soul and heart, and suddenly, it changes you – just like leaven, the mustard seed, and the tares being planted in the wheat. Jesus told the Pharisees, *"You look good on the outside, but on the inside, you are dead man's bones. You're whitewashed tombstones."* This is how corruption gets in us. It gets in us over time, and the very inside of us that was good, true, and pure becomes corrupted. Jesus stated, *"If your eye gate, if your sight is full of light, your whole body is full of light. But if your eye is full of darkness, your eye gate sees darkness, guess what, it's full of darkness."* Matthew 6-22-23.

It is interesting to note that Hitler rose in a country where there were extreme circumstances. The people in Germany were probably good, moral people, and there was likely a large contingent of Christians in that nation. This charismatic leader came along and promised economic renewal and a country rising again. In a depression, people want anything other than what they currently have. He had a way of talking to them, and they bought in. I've watched documentaries that show most people didn't know what was happening with the Jews. I don't know if that's true or not, but for sure, they were under a delusional leader who was deceiving them. This dark spirit had blinded people's hearts so that they couldn't see right vs. wrong anymore. When you can extinguish an entire ethnic group from your midst no matter who they are, and it's okay, you definitely are deceived.

Before we go further, I need you to understand that you believe what you believe mainly because of how you feel at the beginning of the process. I will introduce two scriptures to solicit this further. **Colossians 3:1-2** states, *"If then you were raised with Christ, seek those things that are above where Christ is, sitting at the right hand of God. Set your Affections on things that are above not on the earth."*

Romans 7:22-23 in which we read, *"For I delight in the law of God after the inward man: But I see another law in my members warring against the law of my mind and bringing me into captivity to the law of sin which is in my members."* Notice that the war is in your thought life and affections, which are continually scripted by your feelings through stimulus and response, and by what you focus on around you. **Second Corinthians 10:5** talks about casting down imaginations, which I like to call *thoughts with feelings*. If the thoughts didn't have feelings, would you be warring against them? Of course not! So, we see that beliefs and strongholds of thought are largely built by your focus and the feelings you place on them, which then produces the meaning.

That's how it starts. You are a conditioned-response stimulus being first, then a logical being. Neuroscience has proven this; it is not up for debate. This is the way you were created from the Creator. This is not only about science; it's just that they've proven what the Creator knew centuries and thousands of years ago when He created man. The reality is that you're a stimulus being first, and then a rational being. Your beliefs are built by feelings and thoughts put in you through promise or propaganda and introduced in various ways. Whatever goes in your eye gate gets into your heart, and out of your heart comes the issues of life. Out of your heart flows what you really believe. It is who you are, what is harmonious through your whole being at a cellular level; this is what you believe.

My point in this is to get you to understand that we can change. At the societal level, we can change beliefs by creating an ecosystem with Kingdom culture in it, Heaven to Earth. Through that culture and the ecosystem that's developed, we can propagate new ideas that usher in Kingdom life. We must come in from the darkness, pull our heads out of the sand, realize what's happening, and start fighting now, or we won't have anything to fight for.

For instance, the systems the Creator put in place can have the truth or a lie propagated through them because they are formed the same way through seedtime and harvest. When you sow certain thoughts and actions over time into the entire nation's ecosystem at every level, preaching it, communicating it, living it, giving it to your children, putting it in their school systems, putting it in higher learning systems, it is being modeled in the economic, political, and church world. It then becomes the nation's primary belief system, whether it's right or wrong, darkness or light, truth or a lie. Whole nations are empowered by the truth or taken down when built on half-truths, which are no more than lies. A lie is just the truth that you twist a little bit and get into society. You start propagating, talking about, and preaching it in lower-level education systems and universities, in economics and politics, and arts and entertainment. Suddenly, everyone around you has been raised in a culture and ecosystem taken over by darkness instead of light.

The Creator gave us the tools that darkness uses, which greatly frustrates me. Darkness can't create anything new; the Creator is light. Darkness can only copy and twist what the Creator made and use it for his advantage. This is why Jesus said, "The sons of darkness are smarter than us." It is not because they're technically smarter than us but because they take the world's tools put here by the Creator and know how to use them better than us. They use His tools against us by twisting them and making them dark allies to aid their thought system over that which is right. We have to step in as Jesus taught, being wise as serpents but harmless as doves, promoting Kingdom thoughts and actions that bring about a righteous standard in our nation. We must serve in the spheres of influence that exist to give Him glory and bring deliverance from the enemy's lies to the nation. We can only restore this great nation through a systematic and calculated movement of believers who will lead and bring in answers from the Creator Himself.

Chapter 3

Cloak and Dagger

What if the roadmap for building and establishing the Kingdom of God has been right in front of us the whole time? Has the Master Architect Himself laid out a blueprint for us to follow? Let's look at three parables introduced earlier in this book, which is key when discipling nations. When you look at all three teachings of Jesus, you will notice two primary things in common: The Kingdom always starts in seed form, and it's always unnoticed when implemented in the beginning. The very Kingdom initiation starts somewhat cloak and dagger. Through placing the leaven and sowing the seeds, the soil and the dough have no idea what's living in them, and by the time they find out, *it's too late.* The whole lump is leaven, and the seeds come forth when the right circumstances and conditions arise without either knowing what just happened. This is how we come in through Kingdom thought and wisdom and begin to have answers for the world around us, derailing darkness in the process of His light and wisdom showing up through us. Through these very principles, darkness has systematically ascended in and over the tops of influence in our nation.

Darkness can only copy and twist what's created because it didn't create anything. The original systems and how they work is from the Creator Himself exclusively. The Kingdom is built by and large as Jesus referenced, covertly, just like the three parables Jesus taught. His sons and daughters rise into places of prominence covertly just like the lump doesn't know there's leaven in it until it's too late, and suddenly, it's leavened! Notice that the tares were sowed at night when we slept. The Kingdom is advanced covertly and secretly until the wheat overcomes the tares or the lump is leavened. The enemy has slowly converted our country using these same principles by crafting them around his lies instead of the truth.

Changes in our nation have begun to shift and bring about what's now called the Industrial Revolution, which began in the early 1900s and was a great time of growth in our nation. With the promise of a better life for many Americans, it also brought about people leaving the farm or the family business to chase their dreams in the corporate world. Many left looking for higher wages and the opportunity to work for larger corporations and other people. Until this point in time, most Americans were entrepreneurial, having a family business or working in one because that's how the nation was built. It was the cultural community setting at that time.

We also started raising up the best educational institutional systems in the world, especially at the university level. Most, if not all, the major universities were founded by Christian leaders to better our nation. These great colleges and universities, such as Harvard, Princeton, Yale, and Duke, were planted by believers to educate the nation's youth to be the best in the world at whatever their field or endeavor.

With these events happening in our country simultaneously, we had the perfect storm. The Industrial Revolution, universities being planted to give us the best education system in the world, and our country as a whole is growing into a powerful nation. Our country was beginning to grow into one of the most powerful countries in the world, and it seemed like the blessings of the Creator were being released in abundance to us. Christianity was the most predominant, prevalent value system of the United States of America in the early 1900s.

The foundation and values of our country and the Constitution and the Declaration of Independence are full of the DNA of the Creator, so if we would just govern by them, He would bless our country because, in fact, He has. With this in mind, our nation its people had what I call a value-based system of thought that included truth and absolutes. These were based on the eternal law of the Creator. The value-based system affected our personality and psyche and positioned us more with God, family, and country as the central theme we lived from as a nation. We were proud to be Americans no matter from where our ancestors descended. We became part of the American ideal of life, liberty, and the pursuit of happiness for all, which is at the heart of the Creator for humanity to be free to worship and build life as each person sees fit in their heart.

The universities started to make us smarter. With that, we were educated for many professions, creating competition with others in our chosen profession. There was a shift in this time, and it seemed minor but would prove to be a major pivot point in our nation. We began to adopt and embrace the personality-based value system, which emerged around the 1900s. A group of new thought authors and writers started introducing cutting-edge thought ripe for consumption by the masses in our country. These thought leaders wrote about human potential, the power to change yourself, manifesting your dreams, and many other things. Some of these authors were Emerson, Napoleon Hill, James Allen, and Earl Nightingale.

The power of positive thinking and individual potential became the focus first and foremost. This is important because, for the first time in American history, the masses had access to information in a written format that promised them a clear path to enlightenment and success. The movement in itself was mostly positive in that it introduced people to their potential in new ways they had not realized before, which I believe the Father Himself would encourage. However, it laid the groundwork that undermined the value-based system, which had at its core the Creator first. Now it seemed there were some different paths to ultimate enlightenment and potential that man had found on his own, maybe without the Creator being in the center of life first. (The tree of the knowledge of good and evil was introduced.) At the same time, our university professors were being indoctrinated with this mindset. The educated elite of their day embraced this new thought process in its infancy, and the masses of our young people were put on a steady diet of this thought process. It changed the way we were taught and how we saw the world.

Systematically, we went from a cultural basis of values based on absolute truths with an eternal ideology of life, integrity, and honor in the law of absolutes from the Father's heart. Then we began to embrace the personality potential-type value system, which put man at the center of his world. He or she was largely in control of their destiny and potential being realized, opening a door that allows the education system to redesign our nation's psyche. There's nothing wrong with a positive empowerment message or completing your potential in life. I believe in personal growth and improvement, and I think the Creator Himself wants to see our potential completed in Him. However, the real problem exists in the foundational shift from a God focus to humanity's potential based on a set of practiced principles that can be changed to fit the moment. This slight shift in perspective began the very process of thought that everything is relative and not absolute.

With the personality type values, we moved into the 30s, 40s, and 50s, in which America had one of the greatest booms any society has ever had in such a short amount of time. After World War II, we had the Baby Boomers, and the economy exploded. However, we slowly drifted from a society built on culturally-based values of God, family, entrepreneurism, country, and being together as a community to the Industrial Age when working split many families. Many started to be reeducated by a system of higher learning.

This great group of people called Baby Boomers, which I became part of at the tail end, started a shift in the worldview of America from the end of World War II to the Vietnam war. A war overseas that we probably shouldn't have been in, and Boomers coming of age and testing the societal shift in worldview led to one of the greatest up-heavals in our country. I want you to connect the two. By the time the 60s rolled around, these Boomers had started to graduate from high school and enter places of higher learning. The great communist leader Lenin stated, "Give me the youth of America. Give me one generation of the youth of America, and I will destroy her from the inside." His disciples, who were already well entrenched in the education system, began institutionalizing places the believers planted and raised up to educate the generations with the worldview of a free nation. Ronald Reagan sums it up, saying, "Freedom is never more than one gener-ation from extinction; we didn't pass it to our children in the blood-stream. It must be fought for, protected, and handed on for them to do the same, or one day we will spend our sunset years telling our children and our children's children what it was once like in the United States where men were free." Our Founding Fathers and Ronald Reagan realized that if we don't self-govern ourselves and keep our system of a free nation on absolute values, we will lose our freedom in one generation.

The 60s saw Boomers and a culture of sex, drugs, and rock and roll. For the first time in American history, there was an anti-war era. Heroes returning home after risking their lives and fighting were spat on instead of honored. My dad was one of those heroes. A vast cultural divide between the youth and adults in America occurred. The adults felt the youth would destroy our country, while the youth felt the adults were old and didn't understand war is wrong. These divisions have never been healed.

With open wounds, we moved into the 70s. The economics were crazy. I know because I was born in 1961 and was growing up in the seventies. An upheaval happens, and we're already on the way down to darkness. Our institutions have been taken over by the educated elite who saw that as the way to get the youth of America. They slipped in and started teaching a message of a different kind of freedom, one without responsibility or accountability for their actions. The disciples of Lenin introduced the concept of truth being relative. The anti-God agenda was planted in the boomers' minds and hearts in seed form. The quote from Lenin sounds familiar to what is coming from the universities, *"Our program necessarily includes the propaganda of atheism."* To destroy a free people, you must remove God from their conscious. America begins to be destroyed from within as we raise the next generation of leaders in our country with this prevailing mindset. In the last 50 years, people clothed in flesh but controlled by darkness have sold us this lie that Truth is relative. Truth has versions. Shades of Grey. There is no right or wrong. It's only what *you* think.

This is not a new thought. Do you realize that this started at the tower of Babel back in Genesis when there was a group of people who were one? Sound familiar? Movement? They decided to build a tower to Heaven so they would be great, and others would remember them. In Genesis 11:4, we read, *"And they said, let us build us a city and a tower, whose top may reach into Heaven; and let us make us a name, lest we be scattered abroad upon the face of the whole earth."* It was about them. It was all about sex, drugs, and rock and roll, and it was the "me" generation, expressing "me" at all costs. I don't care about you. There are no morals except what I decide. There is no reality except what exists right now. There is no foundational truth except what I believe, and it's all relative to how I see the world. Does that sound like what started developing with the Industrial Revolution and our educational systems? We went from a value-based psyche in America, based on truth and absolutes, to a society based on personality and individual potential. How "I" can use the system and use "my" unique skills to succeed more than my friend or gain an advantage over him.

The implementation of this system started with the Boomer generation, and we didn't realize it was happening because the enemy had slipped in without us knowing. When light leaves the building, darkness automatically comes. Have you ever been to a large auditorium? When you leave, and the lights are turned off, it's dark. If there are no exit signs or emergency lights, it's very dark. We didn't realize it was slowly happening since we had no people with enough foresight to look in the future. This affected the shepherds, too.

The preachers that came of age at this time were suddenly exposed to self-improvement and marketing personalities instead of value-based and Kingdom-based. They bought into some of the smoke and mirrors as well. "Hey, I can build my church bigger if I market better and my personality is better." It became a competition instead of a community. This is how the frog is boiled in the water. The cloak and dagger and darkness have come in to derail light in our country, and the very foundations of our country are under attack and have been for over 100 years now. Many leaders fell under it, unaware of what was happening, and now what we call preaching, discipleship, and raising up champions has little societal impact in the affairs of our nation and on the seven gates of influence that govern what our nation will be going forward.

If you doubt my assessment, then show me one arena in society that we lead and over which the Father's values are the preeminent thought. Education? Politics? Economics? Hollywood? Media? Does His voice have preeminence in any of these? Light has left the room, and darkness has invaded. Little by little, we've lost this war, and are now marginalized in the very nation the hand of God helped to birth. I want to address the concerns of some who will have more overt ministries, such as pastors of churches and those who find their life's calling within traditional church ministry. I believe wholeheartedly in your calling to obey God the way in which you are called. We must have the local church ministry for sure, but in this writing, I'm talking more about the discipleship of nations and how the Word of God addresses this thought and guides us in accomplishing it.

Derailing darkness in our nation and gaining influence in the gates that govern our society is primarily done while cloaked and slipping in unnoticed. Why? Because we have allowed the world to dictate the narrative in our nation for so long that we have lost most of the influence we once held. We must regain our influence or pay the ultimate price. Lenin said, "If you give me the youth of America, one generation, I'll destroy her from within." Don't think this hasn't invaded the highest places of influence in our nation? How about this one? Saul Alinsky discipled Hillary Clinton and Barack Obama. Saul Alinsky, a self-described community organizer, influenced Clinton and Obama through his teaching of how to gain control and power. Alinsky taught them that we get there and control at all costs. The end justifies the means, no matter what it is. In one generation, this obviously flawed thought has worked its way into our political systems at the highest levels. (Alinsky's Rules for Radicals.)

Study it yourself and read some of the material he produced, and you will see this is what he taught and did. We don't care how we get there. It doesn't matter the path. If we have to kill people to get there, no problem. That's what communism does. When Stalin and Hitler rose to power, they used fascism and communism to control the masses. The people they knew were against them were executed immediately, and their families were killed. Although those around them saw it happening and didn't like it, they didn't do anything. Desensitization starts a little bit at a time.

When light leaves the room, darkness invades. Our light has become dim. Our leaven has become weak because we've been fed milk instead of powerful transformational thoughts. We are the sons and daughters of God, and we are to go in and have answers to fix the wrongs that darkness has imposed on our nation. None of us think like that. Why? Because we are a product of our education, whether in the church or the world. Both have been complicit in laying the foundation of this one-world system to bring us to this tipping point.

I've talked about what I think happened in the last hundred years. If you're in America, 40 years or older, and you think this is up for debate, look at what has happened in the last 20 or 30 years. Ask anybody who is a shepherd, pastor, or preacher. Thirty years ago, were our values and beliefs more based upon Kingdom compared to today? Show me in any institution, in any sphere of influence, media, Hollywood, politics, economics, family, or church, where the Kingdom is being established at the top of influence, and the Kingdom's values are the spirit over that mountain or sphere. Show me where that's the prevailing heart attitude of a particular sphere of influence or mind-molder of society.

Do you think darkness does not know how to use these tactics? Do you not think that the enemy has slipped in unnoticed? Did they come in as sheep that were wolves inside? Jesus said, *"They're actually wolves in sheep's clothing."* Do you not realize this is what's going on?

I was talking with a business acquaintance about his church and pastor. He's a nice guy and has one of the largest churches in the Raleigh area. I said, "Well, let me send you a couple of my talks. But I warn you; this isn't the powerless hyper-grace nonsense that's currently being embraced." He said, "Send it. I'm sure I will love it, and my pastor will as well." Then he tells me that he wouldn't be able to preach it on Sunday because it would offend too many people. I asked, "What do you mean he can't preach it on Sunday? What can he preach?" "Well, if he preaches anything that has any form of conviction, discipline, and or instruction by the Word of God that will cause any pain or discomfort for the people, they are usually offended."

So, we see that darkness has come in through by not wanting to hear the Truth or having leaders unwilling to teach the whole counsel of the Word of God. Because of this, we have become weak and anemic people. In the last hundred years, we have built a foundation for the one-world system to take over America, destroy our country, and make us slaves like Stalin did in communist Russia and Hitler did in fascist Germany. We're on the brink of having a set of elites with their one world view in an attempt to destroy our great nation, which is why I'm so passionate about this.

If you are asking, "What can I do?", I have an answer. You can invade your sphere with His power and change it. Jesus taught us to be wise as serpents but harmless as doves. He also taught us how the Kingdom works: like the dough being leavened, the seed being planted in the ground, and the tares sown at night. When no one expects it, suddenly the Kingdom comes in through you and what you have sown. Remember the words of Edmund Burke, "He that does nothing because he can only do little has made no greater mistake." It sounds like Jesus to me, "He who is not faithful with little will not be faithful with much."

We live in a time when believers are marginalized. If you stand up and speak against the ills of our world and speak any truth, it doesn't matter that you say it with love. Others hate you for it and think you're out of touch with what's now. You're either a bigot or a religious fanatic. If you mention killing babies or homosexuality, you're a homophobe and against women.

I want you to see what Jesus taught His disciples. Jesus showed up during the greatest apostasy that had ever existed on earth. The Pharisees came to power between the end of Malachi and when Jesus showed up roughly 400 years later. There were a little over 200 laws and ordinances in the original Law of Moses. The Word of God specifically says don't add to what He says, and don't take away from what He says. In other words, if you add meaning to the word that's not there, you have committed a sin of commission. If you don't address the meaning there, you have a sin of omission. Either way, God's not good with you changing His Word.

By the time Jesus showed up, the Pharisees had added roughly 400 more laws and ordinances. The greatest apostasy was happening because His leaders and representatives were not doing their job or maybe doing it too well by taking liberties that were not theirs to take. In essence, light left the room, and darkness showed up and invaded it. The people who should have been teaching the masses about who God is. The Rabbis were under the influence of their thoughts and ways, which led to their eventual fall from grace. The spiritual leaders of the day were not doing their jobs well, and it affected the whole nation. Does that sound familiar?

If you don't think we're in one of the darkest times in the history of America, losing the battle waged against us, you need to pull your head out of the sand and look around. I'm not talking about your particular denomination and belief, whether you're Baptist, a Methodist, or Charismatic. Those are all labels we've allowed others to put on us. I'm attempting to convey that we have lost our way as the people of God in every sphere of life in our nation. We should be engaged in making a positive Kingdom impact in the world around us over every gate of influence. Instead, we have bought into a limiting world view that either has no power to change our world, or we are in the group who's attempting to leave. I believe we must step in as the people of God and fight for the change needed in our nation right now.

When Jesus showed up, it was arguably, as most of the Biblical scholars will say, one of the most incredible times of apostasy or falling away from God in the history of Israel. I think we're there now in the history of the United States. When Jesus came on the scene, nobody was celebrating Him or His disciples. Instead, they repeatedly attempted to kill Him because His power and authority continually challenged anything the Father wasn't endorsing. Get the picture? We must realize the Father hides Jesus for His whole life until He is thirty years old. No one knew who He was until it was time, as ordained by the Father. He was cloaked until the Father revealed Him to the world.

The chief cornerstone the very temple is built on entered and **was rejected by the establishment.**

Do you realize how the enemy enters? In Jude, one of the first attributes the scripture shares is how the enemy will enter the church. They slip in or creep in unaware in an unexpected way. They weren't with you, ever, but they slipped in like the tares planted in the wheat. Jesus was teaching His disciples when He stated in Matthew 10:15-16, *"I send you out as sheep among wolves."* Notice that the world is wolves, but the very religious leaders of their day were also wolves because He called them *"whitewashed tombstones."* He said there are dead man's bones in your bodies, which is not good. *"Therefore, be wise as serpents, harmless as doves but beware of men, for they are going to take you before councils."* Jesus was teaching His disciples, the apostles, who became the beginning of a movement to disciple nations. They were empowered by the Holy Spirit and started moving into cities. Acts 17:5 says, *"They had so much power in them that wherever they went into cities where darkness was, it would disrupt the whole city, and it would be turned upside down."* How many believers do you know like that today? Jesus himself said, *"You have to be wise as serpents because you're as sheep going among wolves."* If they know you're as sheep, they will eat you immediately. He continues, *"Beware of men because they're going to take you before councils. Scourge you, beat you, and possibly kill you."* You will die in the beginning because they're wolves and you are as sheep. I'm using "as sheep" because that's how Jesus taught it.

I believe He placed it in the scripture like that because our true identity after His resurrection would be Lion cubs in training. He is the Lion of the Tribe of Judah, and we are to look like Him in this life.

In the end, you're going to die because they will drag you before councils because of what you've been preaching. He says, "Be wise as serpents." This has been missing from the church. "Being wise as serpents" was the protype of the early church because the Master himself taught them this is how to be successful in the world and discipling nations.

Jesus makes this statement to show us how to disrupt systems not in line with the Kingdom to empower and release His people to start bringing light into them. Then, the Holy Spirit would begin to be the prevailing heart attitude over the sphere of influence you enter. The majority of believers will not be in a traditional ministry role, meaning they aren't called to lead a church in what's considered pulpit ministry within the local church structure. 97% of believers will have other life callings in the world and more of a covert ministry. In many cases, God hides them in places for specific and strategic things He's doing, where they become the leaven of the Kingdom in society. Through the word, God covered people and placed them in the world until it was time to reveal them.

Jesus, our prototype, was hidden all His life. Joseph was hidden in prison. David was hidden in the pasture while taking care of his father's sheep. No one knew who David was except God; his father didn't even invite him in when the prophet Samuel came for dinner. Moses was hidden as a baby and later in the desert for forty years before he was revealed. This theme runs throughout the Word of God and is still how the Father does it today in discipling nations.

Although this is a theme throughout the Word, Jesus is the protoype. He's the master. He's the one we should be looking to as author and finisher of our faith. Why was He hidden as a young child? Because Herod was killing all the children, knowing a prophesied King was coming. Nobody knew who He was. He was hidden till when? When it was His time that the Father appointed. However, when He came up out of the water, and the voice from Heaven said, "This is my Son, in whom I'm well pleased," the entire realm of the spirit knew who He was then. All the demonic had been looking for

Him. They knew who He was now. He would no longer be cloaked. We see in His teaching that He taught His disciples to do the same thing He had done all His life. Don't let people know who you are until the Father tells you it's time.

When you go in their midst, you need to be wise as serpents. Operating in the wisdom Jesus talked about will keep you alive. Don't reveal the dove or the Holy Spirit until it's time. He stays hidden inside of you until you rise through the wisdom that the Father gives, which Jesus talks about in this passage of scripture. When you begin to have answers for the world around you, then you will start having influence and favor in the arena you are called to lead. In the classic leadership book, "The 21 Irrefutable Laws of Leadership" by John C. Maxwell, the law of influence states that the answers you bring actually gives you influence and favor for you to lead. You will begin to release the dove through the presence and power of the Holy Spirit.

Jesus teaches His disciples to be wise as serpents in the world. Why? Because most people don't care about your God; they only care about themselves and are looking for people who have answers for their lives. If you have those answers, they'll listen to you. Suddenly, you will rise because you can answer others' questions. Trust me, the wisdom of the Father has answers for people's problems, and Jesus said this is the way you do it. Don't reveal you're a dove or a sheep to people when you go into the world. If you do, they will eat you. Jesus was hidden His whole life until it was time. This is a prototype of how the Kingdom is built in the world system and should be over every nation. It's called leaven the lump, tares in the field with the wheat, and the seed of the mustard tree, the smallest among seeds, but yet grows to be the largest tree. Remember, it's not only about saving souls, but His end game is about saving and discipling whole nations.

In the larger part of ministry, it is applicable to use the 80-20 rule. If we disciple nations with the thought of the Kingdom, it would be a

CLOAK AND DAGGER · 39

lot easier to save people in masses. Instead, we go after people trying to get save them in masses, but we never disciple and change their nation. The very nations they live in are still under poverty, under the curse of darkness. Darkness is laughing at us while we get a few people at the bottom of a tree when we could have the whole tree— the nation and the people.

I began realizing that to go up the mountains and up the spheres, and to influence media, Hollywood, and politics, we must have answers for the world's problems. Cloak and dagger involves slipping in unnoticed so that no one knows you're there. The leaven of the Kingdom slips in the loaf, and the loaf doesn't know the leaven is there. As the heat hits the yeast, the leaven causes it to rise without the yeast knowing it's the cause. The Kingdom works the same way; we slip in unnoticed. We start sowing wheat instead of tares and putting leaven in the lump. We put the mustard seeds of His Kingdom in the ground instead of the seeds of unrighteousness. This is how the Kingdom of God works.

Let's look at another parable of the Kingdom in Luke 16:8. He is talking about the unjust steward. It says, "The Master commended the unjust steward because he had dealt shrewdly, for the sons of this world are shrewder in their generation than the sons of light." Why is that? Because the sons of darkness know how to work the systems of the world to get the result they want. Why don't we?

The Father, not the enemy, put all the systems of the world in place to bless humanity. The systems of economics, politics and family, and institutions of media and government were put in place by the Father. He's the greatest artist of all time. The Devil doesn't create anything. He only perverts the things that the Father created. The wisdom of the serpent was from the Father, which is why Jesus said, *"Be wise as serpents."* In Ezekiel 28, you'll find out that Lucifer had a seal of perfection, and was full of a sum of wisdom, perfect in beauty. Where did all that come from? That's right, it came from the Father.

Let's summarize what Jesus is teaching here. **Number one**: Be covert and wait on His timing. Realize that the wisdom of the serpent comes from the Father. It's His wisdom, not the serpent's. But use the serpent's style of cunningness, sagacity, and shrewdness to move into the world and come in unnoticed in the beginning. Jesus came in unnoticed. People had no clue who He was until the Father announced Him. **Number two**: Be shrewd like the sons of darkness who were commented by the master in the story of the unjust steward; in other words, be wise as the serpent on the outside, but the dove is on the inside. Don't release the dove until it's time, but rather gain influence and favor by the answers you bring in this life. Then suddenly, there will be a time when the Father says, *"Okay, it is time."* Joseph interpreted that dream. David killed Goliath. Moses came forth as the deliverer. Samson came on the scene with power and defeated the enemy, the Philistines. Esther went to the king and saved her whole nation. These people were set up for such a time as this. Are you being set up to save your nation, city, or community? That is my question.

Will you step in? *"But you are a chosen generation, a royal priesthood, a holy nation, a peculiar people."* (First Peter 2-9a). We are very different from the world mentioned in the passage above, and as we enter the marketplace unnoticed, we bring in the Kingdom seeds and sow them in the tares. This is how you operate being *in* the world but not *of* it. First, get your foot in the door by looking similar to them on the outside. It sounds like slipping in unnoticed as Jesus did. Jesus says, *"Be wise as serpents."* Why? Because the world is full of wolves or serpents. Notice, this is the tactic that the world uses. They're getting it from the Bible, but they're using it for darkness. Your hammer in the wedge, narrow end first. As the saying goes, *"Allow the camel's nose beneath your tent and it's whole body will soon follow."* Be wise as serpents. Be shrewd as the sons of darkness. Be smart like them. Use sagacity and regality to your aid and don't reveal yourself until the Father's time is appointed. Be covert. Come in unnoticed.

The Book of Jude

I believe the insights and power to disciple nations lies in the Word of God, and He's revealing it to us in this time. Below are some thoughts out of the book of Jude that will assist us. These are so powerful because they provide several things you can apply when we go into the world system. The counterfeit is revealed easily by seeing the original; with this insight, let's look into the book of Jude.

First, in Jude, it says they crept in secretly unaware. The Kingdom is like leaven in bread. You come in unaware. You slip in the side door so to speak. It's throughout the Old Testament, but Jesus Himself slipped into our world unaware and was not announced until He was 30 years old. He's the master, and He's teaching His disciples and us exactly how to be effective and gain influence in the world. When you come in, you come in being wise as a serpent. You don't reveal your true identity until it's time, and you don't release the influence of the dove until the Father says too. He said in Luke 16:8, *"Be shrewd like the sons of darkness."* This is how He's teaching His disciples. That means us, too.

Second, the enemy in Jude perverted grace. So, what do we do? We begin to operate in *the opposite spirit*. We start sowing grace. We start sowing the very thing that has been perverted when people don't understand what's happening. The perversion took time to sell a little at a time. The Kingdom takes time to develop, so you do it a little at a time. It's the same principle. Instead of perverting grace, we go in and grace the place. Grace is best defined as God's empowering presence, empowering you to unpack His reality to them in a way that they can receive it without them necessarily knowing that you just released His presence. The leaven of the Kingdom is put into the lump in the same way, and then, without knowing it, the heat hits the dough, and it has been leavened.

Third, the enemy caused other's beliefs to change – they did not believe in Jude, and were sowing unbelief in the hearts of the people.

In other words, the wrong leaven – the leaven of darkness instead of the leaven of the Kingdom. For us to change that trend, we have to sow belief in people's hearts through words, phrases, and actions. It must have its foundation in the values of the Kingdom to provide them with the best of what God is attempting to give them. It's the Anointing that removes and destroys the yoke. When you start rising like leaven in the dough, in your mountain, you will be anointed with phrases that may not be in your normal Christian language but would be fit for the world and brings people the answers the Father has for them. The wisdom coming through should always be in line with the values of His Kingdom and the Word of God. You do realize that God speaks in more than just your Christianese, right? I've seen this happen in my own life. God will reveal Himself when it's time, and you'll know it. Just by you being there, He will touch people. We have to start changing beliefs by sowing the Kingdom seeds into the people we are called to serve.

Fourth, it's interesting that when light leaves the building, darkness automatically enters. In this chapter, it talks about the angels leaving their first estate. They were put under chains and darkness because they left the light of their original place. In other words, they didn't keep their position or authority. When Jesus left, He gave the keys of the Kingdom to us, His light, to enlighten the nations of what He has already done for them. He said, *"Go and disciple nations."* My question is, which nation in the world looks like it's been discipled? Which nations have the Kingdom values as their foundations, from the top down, and in which the whole nation has been affected by it including their economics and policies? America, at one time in her not-so-distant past, attempted to fulfill this calling of discipling nations and being a light set on a hill; but over the last 50-100 years, our light has dimmed.

We have failed at that job, and it is time to rise up and do it. But notice that the way to do it is to set yourself back into authority. You were made to rule with Him and start rising up the spheres by His positioning and authority in the Kingdom, in the arena of your particular calling. Don't leave your dwelling place; that's what it said. They left their dwelling place. What's a dwelling? The place you live that connects people with His heart. We've left the room, so darkness invaded. We've vacated our position and our authority in the world and who we are supposed to be. He left us in charge to change the world after He saved us. He put the salvation for all people in the atmosphere of our earth. We're supposed to change the world now for good. That's our job now because that was His job. He left, and He left us in the room. Over the last 100 years, we have vacated our position and our authority, and we're not in our dwelling place. Now all we have to do is reinstitute that and step back into our position and our authority.

Fifth, the darkness and darkened sight come in through this perversion of grace, which causes slavery. We have to step back in with light. He's the light of the world, and so are we. We have to step back in and shine the light, and it will have freedom tied to it. For freedom's sake alone, Christ set us free. Freedom is the antidote to slavery and darkness. Darkened sight is a part of the delusion that comes from us vacating the room, and darkness invading people's thoughts inside. This is what it talks about in Jude. We have to step back in and start releasing light when people don't even know it's light, and as the light gets brighter, it's easier to release more of it through the position of authority we hold in the sphere in which we are located. Suddenly, the leaven in the Kingdom starts mushrooming and getting bigger, like a snowball coming down the hill.

Sixth, the enemy comes in and causes you to defile the flesh, meaning your lifestyle turns into that of the world. You start embracing things that you shouldn't. The Pharisees rebuked Jesus about His disciples not washing their hands, and He tells them, *"Look, it's not what's on the outside of the body that defiles a man, but it's what comes out of the heart."* These people came in unnoticed. They sow tares by programming evil into us by different avenues of darkness in the airways, like media, arts, and entertainment. It goes into your eye gate, down into your heart and little by little destroys the very soul and value of our nation.

How do we change it? That's easy. You start empowering flesh. David said in Psalm 84:2, "*My soul and my flesh longed after you.*" You start pouring Kingdom and leaven into your own heart and soul so that there's an anointing on you when you go around people. You pour life into people's flesh and empower it. If the issues that are flowing out of your heart are pure and the light that is coming out of your eyes is total light, then you are on His path, and the world system won't have any place in you. Now it's time for our light to come in the door and go with the wisdom the Father gave the serpent and use it for their good. This must happen to change our nation.

Finally, the last point is that they reject all law but their own. In other words, they become a law unto themselves and believe that what they think is right no matter what and build a life of relativism instead of Kingdom. There's only one law. There's only one Kingdom, the Father's. We go in with His anointing, His authority, and His positioning and start sowing the leaven, little mustard seeds, and wheat among the tares. This is what the wisdom of the serpent does. He's doing it to us. It's time to reverse the curse and do it to him and turn these tactics on him. If we would teach this and give people practical understanding, we could send champions to the mountains and change the world. Lenin said, "Give me one generation of the youth, and I'll destroy America from within." I believe that if you give me one generation of youth, I'll restore America from within.

The question is, will you step in? Would you be one of those champions who changes America, who pulls her back to her foundation? Would you be a new kind of leader who stands for what made our nation great?

Chapter 4

Reverse the Curse

Releasing Answers from the Father that the world is asking is one of the keys of the Kingdom in Reversing the Curse. I believe when you look at the life and teaching of Jesus. You will find that He was interested in answering people's questions, except those asked to manipulate Him. At this point, we go into the marketplace in the world around us, and the places we're called to be leaven and start ascending up the spheres of influence to which we are called. When we begin to have the answers the world is longing for, we will gain influence and favor because of the problems those answers from Heaven solve.

It's interesting to me that Jesus taught his disciples to be wise as serpents. In thirty-five years in the church, I never heard anyone teach on this thought and subject in any depth. If you look at the only description that I can find in the Word of God of Lucifer before he fell, it gives insight into what Jesus was trying to get across in His statement. Ezekiel 28:12-part b says, *"You were the seal of perfection, full of the sum of wisdom and perfect in beauty,"* and in verse 15, *"You were perfect in all your ways from the day I created you."* That's an amazing description of what God created him to be, for His purposes.

Let's take a more in-depth look into this thought. **First,** it says that he was the seal of perfection. Why? This one is easy. The Father, who is completely perfect, made him. As it says in James 1:27, *"Every good and perfect gift is from above, and cometh down from the Father of lights, with whom there is no variableness, neither shadow of turning."*

Second, he was full of the sum of wisdom. In Proverbs Chapters 8 and 9, we read a compilation of what wisdom looks like when it is worked through people and nations. Proverbs 8:2-3 states, "She takes her stand on top of the high hill, beside the way where the paths meet, she cries out by the gates at the entry of the city." Proverbs 8:12 states, *"I wisdom dwell with prudence, and find out knowledge of witty inventions."* Proverbs 8:18 says, *"Riches and honor are with me; yea, durable riches and righteousness."* Proverbs 9:3-part b indicates, *"She cries out from the highest places of the city."* These are just a few verses out of the two chapters, but they are full of promises of what wisdom creates and displays to the world. It puts you at the very top places in the city, at the gates of influence, and as a ruling body. It brings forth excellence and master level creativity in whatever you do when the wisdom of the Father comes through you.

Third, he was perfect in beauty. As I see it, when the seal of perfection and the fullness of wisdom connect like a hybrid, it then produces beauty that flows out of those two and, in the end, brings forth that which is beautiful. When I started getting this insight and revelation, I told the Lord, *"No one will like being identified with the serpent, and even though you said it and taught it, I'm not sure I can wrap my heart and soul around this. Even if I can, how do I explain what this looks like lived out in a very practical way that brings your answers for our nation?"*

I will give you the short version here. In my previous book, ***The Blueprint of God, the Wisdom to Change the World is in You,*** three chapters deal with each subject in more depth. I started with this thought in mind based on being a new creation in Christ: ***All you need is in you now because the Father put it there!*** I believe in your unique DNA from the Creator. There is a destiny, and within you and the calling upon your life, there's also a set of answers that I believe the Father has placed inside of you. As you walk out the call on your life, He will bring you into places of influence to release these answers in His timing for those with issues you are called to solve. In my life, I've found a few things I am good at that bring answers to others around me. I believe the world longs for the answers in **you**, put there by the Father to be unleashed into the world around us and bring solutions that don't currently exist. The foundation for this revelation started in Ezekiel 28:12-15 and Psalms 139:13-18. We will focus on Psalms at this juncture. *"For you formed my inward parts you covered me in my mother's womb, I will praise you because I am fearfully and wonderfully made; Marvelous are your works and that my soul knows well."* *"Your eyes saw my substance being yet unformed, and in your book, they all were written. The days fashioned for me when as yet there were none of them."* The Father put His substance in you before you were born, which He revealed to me as His DNA, or His fingerprint, upon each person.

Everyone is born with a destiny that God is calling him or her to; unfortunately, some don't find it or Him. He put a piece of Himself in you. The seal of perfection, the fullness of wisdom, and His beauty are in you now. Within your seal are your gifts, talents, and abilities, and right beside them is the wisdom that will flow over your gifts as you work with the Father's design in you to complete them. When the twin powers that He put there start coming through you, it brings beauty to those around you. Answers always bring beauty to those who don't have them. When all of you shows up in your particular calling, God will bring His solutions through you, and answers from the Kingdom will flow into those around you.

When we release ourselves into the world as change agents for good, and we have the excellence of wisdom, we gain favor with people not only because of what we believe but because of the answers we bring. Many times, this favor gives us influence with people who don't always agree with us politically or religiously. As the Ecclesia, we must start to have answers for the world around us that fix issues for which they are unable to resolve or find answers.

When you begin to bring superior answers into the marketplace because of your relationship with the Father, and your answers bring solutions to the world's problems, you will find yourself in the place of favor and influence. The answers you bring to the world are what matters to them in the beginning, not your religious beliefs, gender, or skin color. They won't care about any of that if what you bring has solutions for their lives and the world around them. In most cases, when someone reached out to Jesus for their issue to be healed or fixed, He normally asked, "What do you want?" or "What would you have me do for you?" (Jesus was interested in what they wanted.) My question is, are we really interested in the answers those around us are seeking?

In Mark 11:45-47, when a blind man heard Jesus was coming through town, he began to cry out to get the Master's attention. You would think it was obvious the man needed healing for his sight. But Jesus didn't assume that; He asked him, "What would you have me do for you?" The world isn't necessarily interested in our God because we presume to know what they need or want from Him without caring enough to ask what they want. What if we cared enough to bring the best of the Father to them?

Instead of bringing answers to a dying world, we've used the same three tactics in some form to win people. I want to go on record and say that I'm not against any of these, but I think God has a better way. **First,** we've tried to argue people out of Hell into Heaven. While our intentions are good, it hasn't produced the results God is looking for, which is not only saving individuals but whole nations. **Second,** we think that protesting against entire institutions and people in these places will somehow convert them to righteousness and finding God in the midst of our protest. **Finally,** when the first two don't work as well as we hoped, we hit the streets to march about some cause our hearts burn for to bring attention to and change an injustice we see. I want you to understand that these might have a place in the process, but these alone haven't caused major changes in our nation in my lifetime. Why? Because of a lack of the Father's influence through His people at the tops of the gates of societal evolution. I stated early in this book that the people of God must be raised up and begin invading the spheres of influence that are currently discipling our nation if we want to see change.

The main reason these three tactics don't have the long-term impact we would like to see is that all three try to push change on people from the outside in. People never change on the outside until something inside their hearts change. We have attempted to clean the cup from the outside in. Jesus said, *"You have to clean it from the inside out."* He told the Pharisees, *"You are worried about my disciples not washing their hands. It is not what goes in your mouth that defiles you, but it's what comes out of your heart, what proceeds out of your heart are the issues and forces of life."* There's a better way to win people and whole cities, states, and nations. Transformation at national levels must be done in layers, from every angle and inside every sphere of influence.

We must look at ways to bring national reform instead of what we've attempted, which I believe has mostly failed. We need to gain national influence again as believers. Think of something that you believe has brought great fruit and change in our nation. Whether it's an argument to convince people, a protest against something unjust, or a march supporting great things, can you give me any measurement at a national level that the laws have been changed for righteousness over the last thirty years? We will start with the unborn. Are they safer now than they were thirty years ago because of any of these? Are the family and the divorce rate better or worse? Is the debt of our nation better or worse? Are the morals portrayed on TV better or worse? Is our education system at every level better or worse? Are politics better or worse? Can you give me anything that points to a more righteous nation in any area or sphere of life in America? We have lost all the high ground over the past 40 years or so. Why? Because we are somewhat delusional in the church world today if we think His Kingdom values are prevailing in any sphere currently in our nation.

We don't have the impact that we think we do. Things would look different in our nation if we did. Because we are involved, and we win a few battles, we assume our efforts have a much larger impact than they do. Our perceptions are skewed, and we think that great strides are being made, which puts us in a very dangerous position. Show me any sphere of influence in our country that is predominantly filled with our values as a people and in alignment with what the Father desires. We have treated mental ascension as the truth and the results we perceive that we are producing as the same. Let me explain the difference.

Looking at this a little deeper, as a culture, let's say we are introduced to a new set of principles for leading a company or a new way to eat that's better for us. After we read and digest the material and mentally agree with it, we then assume because we have agreed with it, that it's now a working part of our lives, and we must commit to it wholeheartedly. We can teach it to our friends and family as if we own it. But if you haven't taken any new action or experienced the result of what you've learned, then it is no more than mental ascended knowledge. If you don't take any new actions, then you don't own that truth, and no change has really happened.

If you truly believe something, you will take new action and experience the byproduct of that change. Most of the truths we believe so strongly and think are foundational in us are usually no more than mentally-ascended beliefs. They never get down in our hearts, which Jesus talked about, "If it goes down in your heart, it is what will change you." If it only stays in the mental ascension realm, which is in the soul only, it will never become belief and action simultaneously. Like Siamese twins, you can't separate the two. In our culture, we have divided the two, especially in the church world. We must move from the mental ascension of the Word of God to being a people who can begin to disciple nations by going into our sphere of influence and change it. If we believe something, we must take new actions; if we don't act, we really don't believe it.

Just like in Jude, we must move in unaware and start ascending the mountain to which you're called. If you have the wisdom from the Father and you go in being wise as serpents with the insights of the Dove, the Holy Spirit flowing through you, and the answers from the Father, the world is attracted to you because His beautiful answers are revealed. When that wisdom begins to flow through the natural giftings sealed inside you, it produces a beauty on you that gives way to His expression for others. Finally, they meet the Father and His goodness towards them for the first time.

One of my mentors calls it the "sticky factor." It causes you to have favor with people because you have answers like Joseph, who stepped in to solve the Pharaoh's problems. He was appointed second in command in front of everyone. He was put in charge of the world's largest Kingdom, the biggest national amount of wealth at that time that ever existed. Imagine coming into America with answers to fix our debt! Suddenly, you would find yourself before the President of the United States because you have those answers.

We see in 1 Corinthians 1:30, *"But of him you are in Christ Jesus, who of God is made wisdom to us."* The wisdom of the Father flows through us, causing us to rise as sons and daughters of the King. The Word of God promises us in Deuteronomy 28:13:

- We would be the head, not the tail
- You should be above, not beneath
- You should lend, not borrow
- You should be the people who govern with His heart for the nations
- You should be the people of authority

- You should be setting in the gate where His influence is being released over your cities
- You should be excelling in life and business, so, therefore, you have an audience before kings and not obscure men

The influence and favor you receive will ultimately come from the answers you bring to the world. If you don't have superior answers and excellence in what you do, why would others listen to you? Whatever you do in your occupation and calling, if you do it well, you bring answers. Some of that comes from your natural gift, your innate ability, which is in your seal of perfection and flowing over some of the wisdom that He put in you before you were born, according to Psalm 139:14-16. You're beautiful to people because you have answers. If people bring me answers, they're attractive to me. We don't use that term, but that's what it implies.

Jesus taught his disciples two things that will make you successful in the world: be wise as serpents and harmless as doves; and only release the dove or the Holy Spirit when it's time. When is the time to be revealed? It's time when the Father says it is time, for example:

- Joseph stepped onto the scene and saved two nations from starving when it was time.
- Jesus stepped onto the scene of history to bring us back to the Father when it was time.
- Moses stepped into a nation to be a deliverer when it was time.
- David came to national fame when he killed Goliath when it was time.
- Samson stepped in to save his nation from the enemy when it was time.
- Gideon stepped in from nowhere. He was hiding but he stepped in when it was time.
- Esther stepped in when it was time.
- Deborah, Jehu, and Elijah came on the scene when it was time.

Some of these had more overt ministries.

If that's who you are, then do who you are. I'm not against ministry from the five-fold perspective of being who you are, so your ministry will be more overt. Approximately 97% of us will never stand behind a pulpit and hold the position of pastor, apostle, or prophet in a five-fold ministry in church, but we are called to the marketplace. This is the way it works. We are to ascend the spheres of influence and decapitate the head of darkness, the spirits, and the principalities of darkness. If we do that, the Father will cause us to excel up the mountain and gain more influence and favor with the people.

Can I tell you that most believers will have what I call more *covert ministries* in the marketplace? As I received the insights that brought answers in my sphere of influence, I began to have favor that opened doors because of the answers I brought. Here's what Jesus taught – to be wise as serpents! Usually, you can't tell the difference on the outside between you and them; but remember, the dove lives on the inside of you with answers for the world. So, here's my question: Why have we lost most of the high ground in our nation in every sphere over the last 40 to 50 years? We have the biggest churches ever in America, and seemingly more people going to church than ever. Why are we losing our nation to darkness? Where is the America of my youth that honored God, Family, and Country as the cornerstone and foundation of our great nation? That America no longer exists or permeates our cultural expression as it once did because we haven't focused on Jesus's primary mandate, which is discipling nations.

What if we started thinking about discipling nations first? What if the Spirit of the Father became the prevailing ecosystem in every sphere and over our nation again, as it was during our founding? The discipleship of nations implies the Father's heart lives through us as His sons and daughters in these spheres: government, economics, education, arts, entertainment, technology, sciences, family, and church. The nation reflects the values of the Kingdom from the top down, and as that happens, the prevailing heart attitude or spirit over that nation becomes the Holy Spirit.

In Chapter One of my book, *The Blueprint of God: The Wisdom to Change the World is in You,* I explain this subject in-depth, but here's a glimpse of what it looks like. When you look at John 3:16-17, *"For God so loved the world that He gave His only begotten Son, that whoever believes in Him should not perish but have everlasting life. For God did not send His Son into the world to condemn the world but that the world through Him might be saved."* The word *world* is mentioned four times, and *humanity* is mentioned once. At first, I thought *world* was referring to mankind, didn't you? Actually, in the Strong's concordance, there are several translations. Two of which mean the cosmos or orderly arrangements, while none of the four translations point to mankind.

Let's look at it in light of what God's word is saying. I want to propose that the cosmos are organic systems of the world like vortex funnels that all have the Father's thoughts flowing in and through them to all of humanity for our good. For instance, the system of Education would teach us reading, writing, math, and the ways of God that work best for us in life. God's laws and how to conduct life from His perspective would flow through the government system. From arts and entertainment, we would get His view of expression and beauty. I believe He created these systems and others to serve us His DNA and ultimately give us His heart in how they should work from His perspective.

When the spirit of the Kingdom is over your business and home, it's easier for your children to see God and His plan, destiny, and purpose for their lives. What if the Spirit of God becomes the prevailing heart attitude of a city? You've heard from past revivalists that when this happens, whole cities get saved. Why? Because the systems that God put in place from the beginning have been restored to represent His intentions for humanity. This is what Jesus taught. He said once you disciple a nation, you have the spirit of the Holy Spirit over that nation. It's the prevailing heart attitude, or the foundation of that nation, and offers several results.

- It is easier to get people saved.
- People more easily run into God because He's in the atmosphere of the city, state, and nation.
- It's easier to expand that national sense of prosperity and education and all the things that He extends His beauty through.
- The nations around us will see evidence of the living God blessing our nation and want Him for theirs.

We are called to be sons and daughters of nations because when we were called sons and daughters of God, we were simultaneously seated as sons and daughters of Abraham. His name means father of nations, as we see in Galatians 3:7, *"Therefore know that only those who are of faith are sons of Abraham."* Then, in Galatians 3:29, *"And if you are Christ's then you are Abraham's seed and heirs according to the promise."* What was the promise to Abraham? Nations! Now, we are heirs and invited into disciple nations with Jesus. What? Based on that thought, aren't we playing too small? If we save a particular nation, we get the people, too. It doesn't mean, unfortunately, that we will save everyone. We've been content at the bottom of the world's systems instead of rising to the top of the gates.

What if we started living the mandate of Jesus and began to disciple whole nations, cities, and towns where the prevailing spirit over that nation is the Holy Spirit and began to experience a new renaissance across the entire earth? I believe God's mandate is to do it now! Habakkuk 2:14 says, *"For the earth will be filled with the knowledge of the glory of the Lord, as the waters covers the sea."* Why not now?

Let's give the Desire of Nations His reward. Isaiah 66:8-part b says, *"Shall the earth be made to give birth in one day? Or shall a nation be born in a day."* There won't be any nations born in a day in the millennium, but now is the time to disciple the nations and fulfill the King's mandate!

We have been playing smaller than the people of God should. We were born to bring answers to problems. What if you were perfect in all your ways? I'm not talking about perfection as in you never make a mistake; I'm talking about growing into mature sons and daughters of God who begin to bring His perfect answers for all humanity. What if you bring that into the marketplace, leavening the whole lump, seeding it with the little seeds of the mustard tree? Do you not think it would create an atmosphere of change, a cultural shift, and an ecosystem within your business, company you work for, or the city in which you live? When several people do this, it will create a tipping point in our nation.

In a national sense, the psyche would come under the power of the Kingdom. We only have two choices in what spiritual ecosystem will be over our nations: the power of darkness or the power of the Kingdom. I don't understand why people think it is multiple choice: it's either the Father's Kingdom or the Devil's Kingdom. You have to serve somebody. Even Bob Dylan knows that (pun intended). *Answers release people from the inside out to value you;* it gives you influence and favor because they see you care about them. The Father cares so much about the world He sent His only Son to die for it. When you were still a sinner and could not find the Father because you were separated by Adam's sin, Jesus, the savior of the world, the person who is the Christ, the Anointed one, the Messiah, the Kings of Kings and the Lord of Lords, gave His life for you. He became you that you could become Him and extend the life of the Father now in this life. He did the great exchange when you were a sinner, and we as people were in darkness. The Savior came and gave His life, not knowing if any of us would receive Him.

Think about the sacrifice the Father made. He loved the world so much He gave His only begotten Son. He loved the world, not only people, but the systems He had put in place to serve you: economics, politics, arts, education, family, media, and church. All these systems should bring life and help aid His sons and daughters to live fully alive and free – total salvation, spirit, soul, and body. This is how we change the world.

It happens one person at a time. "What can I do?" you ask. Go to work today with some answers. If you don't have them yet, talk to the Father until you get answers about your company's problems (He will talk to you). Solve it. As you solve problems, "*to whom much is given, much is required.*" You will move up the mountain and get more weight on you, called glory. The Glory of God is man fully alive. People will respond to those who are fully alive will want to be around you. They will care about what you care about if you come in full of life with answers and show the Father cares about them. Do you not think that you are more attractive that way, beautiful as it were? Through your beauty, your answers and being fully alive, suddenly, the Father will say, "It's time to release the Dove." Boom! That one's saved; that city's saved, that nation's saved, your community's saved, children are saved. What if over a high school in America, there is a prevailing heart attitude of the Holy Spirit, and it becomes so well known that it is the best high school in all of America? Because of the Kingdom values, will it not get people's attention?

We underestimate the power of answers, and we overestimate our power to argue, protest, and parade.

I have been in a church for 35 years plus. I look at America now, and I look at how it was when I was 21. America was much freer then.

America was under much less darkness and the one-world system thought. The America I grew up in doesn't exist right now. The only way it will be reformed and have a fresh renaissance is for the sons and daughters of God to step in their place with Kingdom answers, beauty, and the influence answers bring. We must begin to take His mandate up to the top of these spheres and allow the Holy Spirit to be the prevailing heart attitude over the mind molders of society. Until we get this concept out of mental ascension and into the heart where Jesus said all issues flow from, we're not going to change anything. We need to be known for our solutions that fix things that the world is crying out for and engage again in the world with the Father's heart for them. He left us with His authority and power to change the world we live in for good. When we begin to rediscover our identity as sons and daughters of the Father and what He has provided for us in this life, then, and only then, will we find the answers for which the world is seeking.

Let us step into our destiny and change the world with His Kingdom thoughts and values and see our nations become habitations of righteousness. Matthew 28:18-part b through 19 says, "*All authority has been given to me in heaven and on earth. Go therefore and make disciples of all nations, baptizing them in the name of the Father and of the Son and of the Holy Spirit.*" We see He has all authority and power, which He delegates to us and says go. He left everything we need to disciple nations! Let us do it at once.

Chapter 5

Kingdom Leaven:
Tactics of Implementation

I want to start by introducing the thought all shifts in societal evolution happen with small, incremental, almost unnoticeable actions that produce an undercurrent of change. Whole nations are changed from the top-down, meaning that it only takes three to five percent of the population to shift the values and laws that define who we are as a nation. The percentage of people required to change things is determined by their proximity to what they want to change. For example, the United States government is made up of far less than 1% of the population, yet they pass laws by which we must abide. If we want to change things, we must be at the right proximity of power and influence to make those changes and learn how to operate like our Creator. The Creator is the ultimate incrementalistic. He says in Isaiah 28:10, "*Precept must be upon precept, here a little, there a little. Line upon line.*" The Father knows how the end will be a million years before it happens. He is a genius at implementation. The people of God haven't quite understood this concept as much as the world does, so we must begin to be great at implementing the change we want to see in our world.

I want to hit upon some things that hopefully will help us see it a little differently. Let's look at some quotes by Edmund Burke, which will give us the essence of where we are. "All that's necessary for evil to triumph is for good men to do nothing." If you recall, I spoke previously about how all it takes for an auditorium to be darkened is for you to turn off the lights. It is then completely dark. When light leaves the room, darkness invades. In America, we are free people, but freedom has to be given to people who can govern themselves.

Burke continues, "What is freedom without wisdom and virtue? Which is truth, absolutes. It is the greatest of all possible evils, for it is folly, vice, and madness without tuition or restraint." Without tuition or restraint, it is the greatest of all evils. The very thing we as Americans celebrate, freedom, becomes the greatest of all possible evils without self-government. "In a democracy, the majority of the citizens are capable of exercising the cruelest oppression upon the minority." Believers have been systematically minimized over the last 100 years, and for sure, we have become the minority in any cultural reform in our nation.

"The essence of tyranny is enforcement of stupid laws," Burke continues. Jesus taught His disciples when going into the market-place, be wise as serpents. "There is no safety for honest men except by believing all possible evil of evil men." Notice that Burke is saying, in essence, is what Jesus taught. In other words, "Be wise as serpents." Trust must be earned, it's not given. When people come into your life, you need to have boundaries. Wolves usually come in sheep's clothing. In Jude, we read that these men crept in unaware. They look, taste, smell, and talk like you. You can't tell the difference.

Dante Alighieri said, "The hottest fires of hell are reserved for those who remain neutral in times of moral crisis." There is no neutrality. Edmund Burke also said, "Silence is golden, but when it threatens your freedom, it's yellow." "Those who don't know history are destined to repeat it." Jesus taught the disciples using these concepts of what the Kingdom of God looks like when it's lived out properly. For example, if you put just a little leaven in a lump, it leavens the whole loaf of bread. The dough is unaware that leaven is there. If you go into a field at night and sow tares among wheat, they'll grow together. You can't pull one out from the other until it's time to harvest. We should be sowing wheat in the middle of the night, not tares. Jesus also talked about the mustard seed being the smallest of all seeds, but yet when it grows, it's the largest of all trees of that type, and the birds make their home in it. He likened all three of these things as the foundation of how to build and grow the Kingdom of God into a nation's culture.

The Devil cannot create anything new (he can only counterfeit what's been created). Think about it like this – how did he become the father of lies? How did he know what a lie was? The only way you could tell a lie is by knowing the truth first; if there is no truth, there can't be a lie. Without an original, you can't make a counterfeit. The spirit of darkness can only work with the tools and the systems that originated from the Creator's perfect design and blueprint. The Devil has taken the systems and tools already created, reversed them, and used those tactics against humanity for centuries. We need to be wise enough to understand the blueprints and answers for the world's problems: the structure of government, economics, church, and other spheres that influence our lives are in the Word. When we rightly divide His words and wisdom and start understanding how to implement the Kingdom into everyday life, we will start seeing change.

The quotes from Edmond Burke not only inspire me but also challenge me to live my life at another level. I want to share with you what the Word says about implementation. In Isaiah 28:10, the text reads, *"It will be built upon line upon line upon line."* This has been a tactic of the enemy. The enemy has divided the Body of Christ in America throughout denominations and our different beliefs. This denominational spirit emanates from darkness and has separated us. The world will rally together and not take each other down when they have a common cause or movement to accomplish, like the tower of Babel. In Genesis 11:6, the Lord says, *"Indeed the people are one, and they all have one language, and this is what they begin to do; now nothing that they propose to do will be withheld from them."* Notice that they were one with one common language or form of communication, which they all understood. This doesn't mean that they didn't have different thoughts about things. They probably had disagreements, but all had one thing in common. They were going to build that tower.

The world seems to work better together when there is a common initiative to accomplish a goal. We allow our petty differences of doctrinal beliefs to separate us. The church is discombobulated in America with our pet doctrinal differences; we must come together now in this hour. I have been guilty of allowing my view of what I believe to separate me from others in Christ. We don't have that luxury in this moment of history.

To change this, we have to come together. If we stay silent now, we will be yellow. We might be red in Dante's inferno burning. Let's look at an example of small shifts creating massive change over time. It's has been proven over the last 50 years that you can desensitize people to evil. You don't even realize it's happening to you. When you watch stuff over and over again, it goes into your eye gate and your heart. Proverbs 4:23 says, "*Keep your heart with all diligence for out it springs the issues of life*." Many movies and television series allowed in prime time now, labeled "Mature," would not have been allowed to be shown 30 years ago in prime time. If you were to find them, it would be at a movie theater and they would be X-rated. "Mature" has become normal, and we wonder why there's so much perversion in our nation. How about the violence in our youth? We show them killing all the time! What do you expect them to do? We have released a spirit of lawlessness over a generation through movies and TV series, and now we are reaping what was sown in their hearts. Whatever you let in your eye gate goes into your heart. Remember the concept of cooking a frog? We are desensitizing people from light to darkness.

Notice what Dante said, "The hottest fires of hell are reserved for those who were neutral in times of moral crisis." If you don't think we're in a moral crisis now, I don't know how much worse it needs to get to convince you. We are almost to the point of being forced to put three bathrooms in every business now, so transgender people will have their own bathroom. People are confused about whether they're a boy or girl now. Will pedophiles be next? Will we think it's okay for men to marry boys? You say, "That's crazy! It won't happen." May I remind you that people knew who they were based on the body they were born with just a few years ago! Who would have ever thought people would be questioning who they are? Are they another person somehow trapped in the wrong body, unsure if they are a boy or a girl? This is now being imposed upon society; not just imposed but accepted by many.

The point is this is happening. How did it happen to America, the greatest nation on earth? Lenin made the statement, "If you give me the youth of America, one generation, I will destroy her from within." In my lifetime, darkness has been greater at implementation than light has been. I haven't seen incrementalism taught anywhere in church consistently. Why? We don't think like that. Why? We have bought into many beliefs that limit what we think is possible or what we can accomplish while we are here.

Let's look at a couple of these beliefs that I think have all but destroyed our effectiveness. The big one is this spirit of fatalism propagated by people overly concerned with the rapture and leaving than occupying and disciplining nations until He comes. It goes something like this: *We are waiting for Jesus to come back and rescue us from the world.* The other one is the world is going to get worse and worse, as it says in 2 Timothy 3:1-13. Maybe that Scripture is meant to challenge and provoke us to do good work to change it; instead of it being absolute. What if the Father is saying, "*If my sons and daughters would show up, with my power and answers, this might be restored and not destroyed?*" What makes me think I can change the Father's heart on that matter? Simple, I'm a son of God! I have a seat at His table. I'm in the family business because of the finished work of Jesus; everything that belonged to Him now is mine in this life.

2 Corinthians 5:21 says, *"For he hath made him to be sin for us, who knew no sin; that we might be made the righteousness of God in him."* Also, in Romans 8:19, the text says, *"For the earnest expectation of the creature waits for the manifestation of the sons of God."* In 1 John 4:17-part b, we read, *"Because as He is, so are we in this world."* These three scriptures give us a foundation of not only what He did for us but what He intended us to do and be while we wait for His return.

If you are still not convinced that we can change destiny and rewrite history, then let's take a look at people who did. How can a man like Abraham barter with God over Sodom and Gomorrah and convince God that if he could find at least ten righteous people in those cities, He wouldn't destroy it? He'd already decided to, remember? Let's take a moment and think through this story. A man in the Old Testament who wasn't born again convinced the God of the universe to change His mind! Wow! How many of us think that way? Maybe we should. How can Moses stand in front of God and tell Him He's wrong and God repents because He was going to destroy and kill all the people of Israel in one blow? If Moses hadn't stepped in, would they have lived? The answer is no.

The list goes on and on from Joshua asking God to stop the sun from going down to David establishing twenty-four-hour worship around the Ark of the Covenant without asking God if it was OK. How about Elijah in 1 Kings 17:1? He tells King Ahab it won't rain until he says it will again. Gideon required a fleece; Deborah became the only woman judge in Israel; Esther had to go before the king with only her uncle's guidance and no word from the Lord. This short list of saints all have one thing in common: they lived in the old testament, and according to Hebrews 8:6, the New Testament was established upon new and better promises! That means it's superior in every way, with superior promises. My question is this: *How many believers do you know who look like and act as powerful as those listed above?*

When I was challenged with this question by the Lord, I answered "None." How about you?

If it's true that we live in a superior covenant established by Jesus for us to do life exactly like Him, in the here and now, then evidently, we have more power and standing with the Father than we are currently accessing. In my mind, we need to stop making religious excuses because of some twisted view of who we are and our place in history and start changing the world around us! We are the sons and daughters of God! We see in Luke 16:8, "*And the Lord commended the unjust steward because he had done wisely; for the children of this world are in their generation wiser than the children of light.*" In plain North Carolina English, the text says they are smarter than us! According to the covenant that we've been grafted into, we should "*be the head and not the tail, above only and not beneath, we should lend and not borrow.*" (Deuteronomy 28:12-13) How can all of the above be true if the world is smarter than us? Good question.

It's a challenge from the Lord for us to change it; it's a statement to provoke us into leading as He intended. As a people, we have developed a belief that either we are leaving soon, or the world is will get worse no matter what we do. With either of these belief systems, we don't attempt to make a difference. This belief goes against what Jesus taught, which was to occupy until He comes and make disciples of all nations, as we see in Matthew 28:18-20 and Luke 19:13. The problem with this thought process is we keep losing our nation to the world because they don't have this belief. We as a people don't think about how our life will impact future generations. We need to put on the mind of Christ and become incrementalistic, planning, and dreaming with the Father about the next 100–150 years. Then, we will be planning for generations we want to see in this life. The Old Testament is full of this thought, where they list their genealogies of many generations. We should start thinking like this again; this is how the sons and daughters of the King should think. We're too preoccupied with leaving when the world isn't. They're trying to figure out how to get medicine and technology to live to be 150 years old while we're talking about His coming back next year, or how we can't fix it anyway. I've heard this my whole Christian life. I'm not against teaching that Jesus is coming back because ultimately, He is.

The problem is the mindset and the actions that align with this thought process are inconsistent with occupying until He comes. Whatever is in your heart is what you do. If in your heart you think you're leaving, why would you do anything in society to change it? Why would any of us want to go up the mountains to fight and take out principalities or go to the top and have influence if we think the world is going to hell in a handbasket, and it's going to get worse no matter what we do? This is a tactic of the enemy to keep us from making a difference. Thank God our Founding Fathers didn't think like this, or we wouldn't have and live in a nation as free and pros- perous as ours. They wanted a place that was better for their children and their grandchildren than what they had. These teachings in their current state have done more damage to the fulfillment of the great commission and discipling of nations than any other thing in my lifetime.

How did we get talked into this thought? This fatalistic thought that we've developed is not from the Father. It's from the Devil because he comes to steal, kill, and destroy our current identity as sons and daughters of the King and, therefore, removing God's influence through us to change the world. He's desensitized us to not only evil but also good we should be pursuing. We are not doing anything because we don't think it's worth trying. We won't even fight. The Father is this great incrementalistic. But He has to work with the people He has on earth. The enemy has used this against us.

How many believers do you know that talk about what they're going to leave as an inheritance, either spiritual or material things, for generations after them? I met a guy in California about 14 years ago who talked about a 150-year plan. I'd never heard one believer, leader, preacher, or anyone with any influence talk about a 150-year plan before then. It blew me away. This was the first time I had ever heard a preeminent Christian leader talk about this. It sounded like the Jewish culture to me, like the sons of Abraham's generational thought. If you thought that your life's work and impact would exist 150 years down the road, three to four generations from now, would you live differently? Would you plan differently? We must upgrade our current Christian culture and ecosystem.

We need to understand how an ecosystem is built over time. Let's look at the difference between a culture and a complete ecosystem. Culture is best described as an individual development of an area that you propagate. For instance, in a square section, we propagate that area and create a culture or a garden. The ecosystem is the structure of the atmosphere around it, the trees, woods, and other buildings. The ecosystem is all of the development around the individual culture.

I live in North Carolina. As an example, consider a mountain laurel from Asheville that has been planted on a mountain over decades, thriving in the ecosystem developed around it. If I uproot the laurel and plant it in Wilmington, North Carolina, the plant will not survive in that ecosystem. Its culture has been developed over hundreds of years in the mountains. If I remove it from its current ecosystem, it will die. If I take a palm tree from Carolina Beach, where it has developed in an ecosystem of sandy beaches, warm ocean breezes, and salty air, and plant it on the side of the mountain in Asheville, it will die the first winter. This is the difference between a culture and an ecosystem.

His Kingdom answers implemented correctly will cause people to feel differently about what we're bringing and who we are. Jesus is a genius. When He approached people who were calling out to him, His first question usually was, "What would you have me do?" or, "What do you want?" He was truly interested in people and what they wanted. He didn't assume, for instance, when the blind man was crying out, "Have mercy on me, Son of David." He asked him, "What do you want?" He didn't assume the guy wanted to be healed from blindness. He was interested in giving him the answer to his question.

One thing that must change in the body of Christ as a whole is we have to start loving the world as much as the Father loved it. He said that He loved the world so much, He gave His only Son for the world.

The Father is a pragmatist. He is the greatest pragmatist who has ever existed. He can wait for eons for something to happen. He sees so far into the future, trillions of years, we can't even comprehend that. He knows how to plan things. He's a genius.

We as a people have underestimated the power answers have in the world. In most cases, Jesus asks people what they wanted from Him. When we start being the answer for the world, it will change how they feel about us. If you bring something positive for them, then suddenly, the way they think about you is completely different because they associate you with answers to their problems. If I bring answers to you to solve your problems, will you feel differently about me? Absolutely. If I do that consistently, it's called influence and favor. It also conditions within you a positive feeling about me, and possibly create a stereotype that others who are believers would be just like me. Do you see how that changes the way people see you?

The world has tried to desensitize us with God's very on playbook, and it has done a good job. To reverse it, we must bring the sensitive answers to their problems and allow that feeling of, "Oh, I didn't know believers could do this. I didn't know people like you would have answers." I'm not telling you to bring out a calling card that says you are a believer. As I've said before, most influence happens without others knowing who you are until you gain their hearts and have their trust. You will always find the answers to people's problems in the implementation of Kingdom ecosystems. Why? Because the Father loves to engage people through His goodness, which comes in answers many times. We must begin to develop the ecosystem and structures in which the Kingdom culture can grow. You don't have answers for everyone's problems, but you have answers for someone's problems.

Answers are the answer. I've seen this happen over the last decade, most of the time, accidentally. I've been more open to it happening on purpose recently as I've seen this is how His Kingdom enters. Through the life I've lived, I know what I know. But some of the things I know, others don't know. You probably have expertise or you've learned something that not everyone knows. The very natural things you've learned in life can, and I believe will, become a platform the Father will use to answer the world's questions in your sphere of influence. Often, a natural or innate gift or talent you have, which you have been blessed with by the Father, will allow you to answer other people's problems when you are open to Him flowing through you.

Do you realize He cares more about what you care about than you do? This includes answers to questions others around you have. When people cried out to Him and got His attention, He asked what they wanted. He didn't assume He knew. He's the Son of God. He can read the intents and thoughts of men's hearts, period. He could see through people with x-ray vision and yet He asked, "What do you want?" We should be using the Father's tactics when attempting to answer people's problems to give them life. If we create a critical mass in this, the stereotype of a believer will shift and change in our nation's ecosystem and culture. Suddenly, the tide swells toward us instead of away from us, marginalizing and minimalizing us. As you gain influence and favor through answers, you get promoted in life. The more value you add to clients, customers, or people around you, the more promoted you'll be. That's the way the Father set it up, and how it works in the world. "To whom much is given, much is required. If you're not faithful in little, you won't be rewarded with much."

These are keys to bringing you into promotion. As you do, you'll gain more influence and encounter different situations requiring more answers. But eventually, if you do it correctly, you will be at the top of influence, either with the top people, teams, or those who make the rules for that sphere, whether it's education, politics, arts and entertainment, or family. What if through the answers He gives you bring in the leaven of the Kingdom, which can't be seen by the way? I believe tactically speaking, it's answers for people's problems at first. The favor and the influence come next. As that comes in, trust is built, and you can implement more leaven noticeably because they like and trust you. You have influence with them. You have solved a lot of problems for them. Trust me, if you bring that to the table, people won't care about what you believe. This is accessible for all believers and is the primary way to have influence, favor, and gain trust. Not through manipulation, but by giving people answers and not expecting anything in return. Allow the Father to promote you.

This isn't about imposition; it is about influence. The moment you make it about imposition, you will no longer get answers from the Father because He's doesn't do it that way. He wants people to be influenced by His power, His love, His grace, and His glory through His sons and daughters who have answers for the world's problems. As you build that portfolio of His answers, you will attract the world because you don't make it about an agenda. You don't make it about being a Christian or not, your political persuasion, or your skin color. Just think, "I'm going to do the best I can because it's the way the Father is. That's what He does for us." Reveal the Father to people, and conversion happens. We're trying to figure out how to save the people. When the time is right, give them the answer to their problems and tell them it comes from the Father.

He wants us to be that in the world. He wants the Kingdom leaven to get so stuck into the world it becomes the ecosystem that invades the culture of people's lives, which gives the best of the Father to them. This is our job, and the primary way we invade, gain influence, favor, and trust is to build with the answers that are superior to people's problems! You won't have answers for everyone, but you will for someone. God will put you in play with people when you have this heart, and He will start placing you just like He did Joseph. Joseph was in charge everywhere he lived, even in prison. No matter what people did to him, he always rose to the top. That's Kingdom leaven.

Notice that nobody in the nation knew who David was. David wasn't even invited to the party thrown for the great prophet of their day, Samuel, who was coming to Jesse's house. All seven brothers and Jesse were there with the prophet Samuel, but they didn't invite David. His father didn't believe in him enough to invite him to the party. Nobody knew who he was. Yet, when he showed up with answers and killed Goliath, historians say he was about 14 or 15 years old. Goliath said, "I'm coming to you as a warrior, and you send me sticks and bones?" David might have been a little guy, but his answers were big enough to save an entire nation. He went from farmer to king with one answer! This is the nature of Kingdom leaven; it slips in the palace when you least expect it. This is what we're called to do.

Esther slipped in the palace through leaven, and nobody knew who she was. She was born for such a time as this. When the leaven had fully developed and caused the dough in the bread to rise, suddenly, she stood before the king and saved her nation.

We have missed a big part of theology about how we invade, gain influence, have favor, and gain trust with people. I've done the same thing because I didn't know any different. As I've looked over my lifetime, I realized that God is for people. The Father loves people. He loves them so much that He gave His only Son. He wants to save the world, not only the world's systems, but people and nations. He wants to save whole nations. His love is so broad and deep that He wants people to know Him. The way they know Him is to be one with Him. We're supposed to look like Him. Remember, Jesus always asked people, "What do you want?" He was interested in giving people answers to their questions.

I want you to understand that the Father is the ultimate pragmatist. He is about line upon line, precept upon precept, and here a little, there a little. Suddenly, the wheat takes over the tares and the smallest seed, the mustard seed was sown. It becomes the largest tree, creating an ecosystem for the birds to make a nest. The Kingdom of God is like leaven. The dough doesn't see the leaven. The dough has no idea the leaven has slipped into it. Suddenly, the dough explodes, and the Kingdom is made manifest. This is the way to change world – one seed at a time, one person at a time, one community at a time, and one nation at a time when they see the goodness of the Father. The Word of God says, "It is the goodness of God that causes men to repent." In other words, His goodness has the power within it to cause hearts to turn to Him. It doesn't say judgment. It says the goodness of God leads men to repentance. What is repentance? God, you're so good, I'm going to turn entirely from this way of doing life. I'm turning to you because you're good beyond anything I've ever seen. You're beautiful. You are the Desire of nations. You're the lily of the valley. You're the fairest among 10,000. What if we looked like Him? You do realize that's the goal, right? He's the perfect protype; we need to look like Him.

He became you in all your sin and death so that you could become Him and all His righteousness. If He became you, are you becoming Him in this world? Yes, you are. Through the perfect sacrifice and His finished work for us, you became Him. We are little Christs running all over the United States and the world. What should we be running out with? That God is good. He loves people, and He's interested in giving them answers to their problems.

What if we look like the Desire of Nations? What if His sons and daughters started looking like the lily of the valley, the fairest among 10,000? Jesus said, "If you've seen me, you've seen the Father." My question is, if people see us, have they seen Jesus and the Father? That's the way it should be through the finished work. They should be getting answers. Leaven gets into the culture that causes the Kingdom to have the ecosystem over a city; Kingdom should be the overarching ecosystem. The culture is the leaven that gets in people when they see how good He is through the answers you give and the implementation of those answers. Suddenly, they realize that He's the fairest among 10,000, and they want Him because He is so, so, so good.

Chapter 6

Heaven on Earth

I want to explore how Heaven is manifest on earth, and His world begins to collide with ours. In Matthew 6:10, we see the Lord teaching His disciples how to pray, "Thy Kingdom come, thy will be done in earth, as it is in Heaven." In this passage, we see it's His will that His world invades and affects ours. How does that happen? We are left as His light and authority on the earth. If we don't show up, the light doesn't show up.

Darkness only invades a city, community, home, and nation if light leaves the room. Darkness cannot stay where light is, period. In talking about the enemy speaking evil against God Himself, Daniel 7:25 says, *"And he shall speak great words against the most High and shall wear out the saints of the most High, and think to change times and laws; and they shall be given into his hand until a time and times and the dividing of time."* The words of the enemy spoken against God affects us in the earth realm. Why? Because the enemy wants to change times, seasons, and laws. They spoke against the authority of the Father. By doing that, the power of their words came against the saints and is wearing them out. Darkness is wearing light out, which shouldn't happen. He also wants to get us off-kilter, so we don't realize that he wants to change times and laws. Why? So, he can steal, kill, and destroy. It's never to give life.

One of our challenges is that for some reason, we think we can negotiate with darkness. You can't negotiate with evil. We must realize there is an enemy. Paul says in Ephesians 6:12, *"We don't wrestle against flesh and blood, but we wrestle against principalities and powers and might and dominion in Heavenly places."* The evil thoughts that men have in their soul exist because darkness has invaded their thoughts since it is in the atmosphere around them. The leaven of the Kingdom should be invading them by shining our light so bright they can't see anything else. The light of His brightness shining through us and on us and coming into them, so darkness has to leave the room when the light shows up, which is the point.

Edmund Burke stated, "The fate of good men who refused to become involved in politics or the making of laws is to be ruled by evil men." When I was growing up, people didn't talk about politics and religion because it always caused an argument. I think it is time to talk about both, and right now more than ever. Our survival as a nation will depend on us reestablishing a righteous standard in both arenas. We need to become more educated and talk about it more, not less. As Burke says, "When good men decide and refuse to be involved in politics, they're destined to be ruled by evil men." Evil is ruling over righteous people, which is what has happened to our country. We let darkness start ruling, believing the world would have answers for our problems.

The world doesn't have the answers because it only has one tree to go to – the tree of knowledge and good and evil. Believers have another tree living in them called the *tree of life*. If we allowed the branches of His answers to come through us, the world would want to eat the fruit of the King Himself. Even though they might not know what it is, when they bite it, it would be the best fruit they ever had because it is fully alive, full of resurrection life. We have to start engaging again in the marketplace of ideas and answers for our nation's soul or suffer the consequences. We have been backing away from leading in every institution in our country, thinking that the world would have the answers, but they don't. We wonder why we no longer recognize our country. We have backed away, and light has left the room. We must step in the fray and battle for our nation's soul or pay the ultimate price of losing our freedom.

The greatest sin is to do nothing because you can only do little. I love America. It's my home. I'm not a doom and gloom person, and I think that our best days are ahead. But I think we have to do something **NOW.** If you read the parable of talents, you see that the Master of the house gave talents to three different people who were in his house: five, two, and one. Two of them did something with it, were commended for it and were rewarded with more. One of them put the talent in the ground and buried it because he was afraid to do anything; doing nothing because he could only do little. Does that sound familiar? It says he was thrown into outer darkness, where there's gnashing of teeth. That tells me if you do nothing and stay silent when you need to step in, you will be viewed the same way by the Master. I don't want to end up out there.

People often ask me, "What are we supposed to do?" *This book is me doing something.* First, we need to do silence the enemy. You cannot negotiate with darkness. It just doesn't happen. Our aim should be to muzzle and shut down the enemy's tone and voice. He says great swelling words and deceives many. We have to take over the atmosphere of our own beings first and foremost. We must learn how to reach out through prayer and grab those things that are contending for our city's soul and say, "No, I'm here, and I rebuke you in the name of the Lord. You're not going to be in my city." We must do that first and silence the enemy through prayer, declaration, and enforcing the covenant and finished work that Jesus has already put in place. He said, "It is finished." So, all you have to do is step in. He gave the keys to the disciples, saying, "Here are the keys to the Kingdom; go take authority over and disciple nations." The keys have been given to us. He's expecting us to step in and shut down the enemy so people will have a chance to know Him. Darkness is invading the atmosphere and we're not stepping in through the declared victory of Jesus and tearing down the altars of darkness that's been built over the gates of influence in our cities. Colossians 2:15 says, *"And having spoiled principalities and powers, He made a show of them openly, triumphing over them in it."*

Enforcing His mandate on darkness from the Word of God, which says, *"He destroyed all the power of the enemy; He disarmed principalities. He destroyed darkness once and for all."* We have to enforce what He's already done. We don't need to destroy anything. We just have to enforce what's already been given to us as sons and daughters of the King and enforce His mandate upon them; to bind them so they are not active in our cities, homes, and nation. Period. The Word of God says Jesus asked the question in the parable, Luke 18:2-8, *"Will I find faith on earth when I return?"* Before He makes that statement, He gives us the story of the unjust judge. This unjust judge says, "I don't fear God. I don't fear man." He says what he thinks. This little widow woman hobbles into the courtroom every day and puts her little crooked finger in the judge's face and says, "Give me justice." Those are the words you use. Notice that she didn't ask. She came in and declared, "You will give me justice for my family and me." She came in every day, day after day, after day, after day. And the judge finally said, "Give her whatever she wants. She's wearing me out." In Chapter 18, verse 5, *"Yet because this widow troubles me, I will avenge her, lest by her continual coming she weary me,"* notice two things: she kept coming no matter what he said or the way she felt, then, through her contenting for what mattered to her, she wore him out. (We can wear out darkness.)

It's interesting that in Daniel 7:25, the Devil is wearing out the saints. Why? First, he made an accusation against God. That accusation is in the realm of the spirit and it then filters down to us in our psyche. We think God is under attack. Trust me, God is not under attack. This is the deception of the enemy, like he is God. He's not God. He is a fallen angel, and those angels are being held in chains in everlasting darkness. We see in the story that the saints are being worn out. Then, Jesus makes the statement after the story of the unjust judge and the widow woman, "at the end will the Son of Man find faith on Earth?" It gives the indication of what true faith looks like in the face of unjust circumstances and conditions. Evil doesn't compromise and evil can't be talked into things. It's going to rule you, or you are going to rule it. Those are your two options. According to Proverbs 29:2, *"When the righteous rule, the people rejoice, but when the wicked rule, the people mourn."*

Over the last 40 years in America, I've witnessed more mourning than rejoicing. We, as a people, have seen the erosion of our values that in the past, made our nation great; we must revisit them now. We must silence the enemy of our nation now; we must wear the enemy out. We as a people have to go in his face, saying, "I'm enforcing what Jesus has already done because I'm a son, I'm a daughter, and I stand inside of His authority and in Him. I will rebuke you because I carry His authority. He's in me and I'm in Him and you have to yield." We must control darkness in the atmospheric realm of our city first. If we don't silence the enemy, he will silence us; isn't that what's happening right now? We have to get in his face like that widow woman and say, "You will yield because you've been defeated."

Second, we must restrain from pushing and peddling our beliefs onto others until we have favor, influence, and trust. Assuming we have silenced the enemy first, this is the next step. Be persistent like the widow and put your finger in the face of evil saying, "You're going to yield because Jesus has already destroyed you, and I'm here to enforce His destruction upon you." However, I have witnessed many people trying to evangelize for the wrong reasons, being rude and pushy, like a salesman peddling his wares. Salvation and God, the Father, the Son, and the Holy Spirit are not for sale, if you didn't realize that. Our faith cannot be peddled or pushed. As a result, we have cheapened our faith and lowered the standards of the cost of following Christ to satisfy our needs or feel like we are making a difference in life.

Often, Christians get a bad rap because they go into their workplaces and businesses, pushing their beliefs upon people because they think it is the right thing to do. "They're going to go to hell if I don't, right?" I have never won anyone over to Christ by pushing what I believe upon them, by the way. According to Benjamin Franklin, **"A man convinced against his will is of the same opinion still."** If they say a prayer to receive Jesus to get you to leave them alone, are they really saved? Saying a prayer won't save someone if the Holy Spirit doesn't draw them. John 6:44 states, *"No one can come to me, except the Father which has sent me draw him, and I will raise him up on the last day."* Pushing your beliefs on them without the Holy Spirit leading them will not get them into Heaven either. Here's a great insight by St. Francis of Assisi, **"Preach the gospel at all times. When necessary, use words."** 2 Corinthians 3:2 states, *"You are our epistles written in our hearts, known and read by all men."* I believe that as we learn to be in the world with the Father's mandate, we will automatically see many conversions of not just people but whole cities.

You are the leaven of the Kingdom, and when you're with a friend who is unsaved, the leaven is going into them because YOU are there, allowing God access. As we finish this thought, let's look at three primary systems of influence in our nation: Education, Government, and Media.

Education

We must begin educating our youth again about our great nation and the benefits afforded to us by those who went before us. We have to remove any revisionist thoughts that don't tell of our great founding or that perverts and changes so much its meaning is lost completely. Over the last one hundred years, there has been an effort to do both, and those indoctrinated with this belief have done a great job. It is time to take our Education systems back from those who try to remove our way of life. At our founding, this system was placed on an eternal absolute guaranteed by the Creator Himself to ensure we are a self-determining, independent nation.

The socialist and globalist worldview has sought to undermine this and make America into another country under the ruling elite's world control. One of their heroes, Lenin, made this statement in the early 1900s. "If you give me one generation of the youth of America, I will destroy the country from within." Why don't we reverse that? Give me one generation of the youth of America who has a heart that burns for righteousness, and I will restore not only America, but also the rest of the known world. America will once again become this light on the hill. We must get the Father's ways and thoughts back into our school systems. We should take the wisdom of the Father and use the answers He gives us. If we will take His heart in and be genuinely engaged in the process, we might gain favor and start implementing His ways.

We can't do this overnight or even in a decade. This is most likely a 25-50-year plan. Yet, we could implement a lot in a decade. We must gain access through influence in the education systems at every level from preschool to elementary to middle to high school and the universities. We must ascend in these places. We have to remove darkness or anything contrary to the Father's intentions, which always is to bring life.

Government

Let's look at a passage from *The Art of War*. **"Those with supreme skill use strategy to bend others without coming to conflict."** Edmund Burke stated, "The fate of good men who refused to become involved in politics is to be ruled by evil men," and "All it takes for evil to triumph is for good men to do nothing." We have to become involved in politics and government if we don't want to be ruled by evil men. Somehow, we must reengage in the process of answering people's problems at every level, including government. You might not go into government as a profession but do what you can to support those who will represent our nation's founding documents, which I believe have the Creator's DNA all over them. The requirement must be to uphold our Constitution and the Declaration of Independence. If not, then they are not fit for service. As we've read before, Edmund Burke said, "Those who do nothing because he can only do little has made no greater mistake." In other words, **DO SOMETHING. And do it NOW!**

Media

The final system of influence we will discuss is media. The spirit of darkness has used this sphere to propagate his thoughts, which leads to the death of any nation that embraces his ways. Darkness spreads much like the leaven of the Kingdom, a little at a time.

In Ephesians 2:2, He is called the prince and the power of the air. Think about it. What goes in our airways? With the technology we have today, thoughts can be broadcast all over the world in just one moment. The good news is that it's easier for the average person to become a mouthpiece through the many different online avenues we have and make a significant impact in our world. Although some of these platforms can shut us down, we shouldn't let that prevent us from going after what we believe and burn for at this time in our history.

We should attempt to create new sets of platforms that the righteous can access without being censored. Become the mouthpiece of life and answers in your arena of influence. Create outlets and publishing forums to get your thoughts and answers out there. How about starting a publishing business to produce new thought leaders of our day? (That is one of my goals.) How about a blog or a YouTube channel to voice what you burn for on Instagram and other outlets? Obviously, some will go into the existing media, which we need. Don't sit around at this time in our nation's history and do nothing!

How about creating your own website; start writing a blog about leadership or life. The blog could be about something that the Father has put inside you. When you allow what He has put in you to be released through you, it has the leaven of the Kingdom on it to change the world. I'm doing this through an audio series and published books on transformation, and how to be fully alive and living free in business and personal life. His presence is on them and therefore, there's a transformational anointing released when people engage with my material. I'm a transformer. When I get around people, that anointing automatically gets on them, which is one way I release the Kingdom leaven.

You have the Kingdom leaven too. You must find out what you can do to start implementing it. Your blog could be about something for which you have a passion. Publish a book. Create a website. Things can go viral and suddenly, you may find yourself in front of kings. By doing this, we can ascend the media mountain. If we become a mouth-piece of answers and influence and don't make it about our beliefs, we will stand before great men. That's what the Word of God says. Let us learn how to release His nature and communication in this season of great turmoil in our nation.

Communication is not telling people what you think they need to hear. Communication is determining what they most need from the Father and communicating that. It's called the art of listening. It would do us well to practice this when we stand before people with whom we're trying to gain influence.

Once people are interested, you have a captive audience, and you have determined what they most want and need to hear from you. Through the art of listening, you will gain people's hearts and trust. Questions are the key. Go deeper. Let the leaven within the words, communication, and trust level you develop seep and go deeper into them. The deeper the leaven gets, the more people can't get away from it. It starts growing within the dough and suddenly it expands, and God's leaven explodes all over them with His life for them.

Create a coalition of people who want to see our nation restored to its righteous foundation from the Creator. We can start by building around the wisdom and words from Proverbs that will give us a core in which to believe. Here's are a few from the book of Proverbs: integrity, wisdom, discretion, prudence, knowledge, discipline, correction, and instruction. Begin to take these words as defined by the Word of God and create a movement around them. More people believe and think like this in America than those who don't. We are discombobulated because we tend to let our beliefs divide us **instead of letting the code of righteousness reign over us.** In Proverbs, the Word says, "When the righteous rule, the people rejoice." Paul even talks about when the Gentiles, who did not know the law, did what is right, they became a law unto themselves. Justice is the great barometer, and it shows that we can create a just society with people who are believers, and those who are not as well. Creating a coalition of justice and righteousness is about a foundation of saving America and getting our country back to a foundation that cannot be shaken.

We must have fresh insights for our nation from the Father again and remove anything that would hinder us from restoring Old Glory to her righteous foundation. We must develop new thoughts, answers, and ways of implementing our beliefs without pushing them on others. For a new awakening and reformation in America, we must believe. The world we live in now is unsustainable as a nation. For the new, we must believe God will give us ideas or insights that cause newness. We must speak that as a mouthpiece and a doer, finding answers people can receive from the Father to improve their lives. Darkness has invaded and is taking the high ground in our nation. It's time to take it back.

We must make darkness and its plight on our people intolerable.

Chapter 7

Thy Kingdom Come Ecosystem

Let's discuss how to build an ecosystem; thy Kingdom come. As a holy nation within a nation, we must revisit the foundation of absolutes of the Word of God and allow His Divine Providence to lead again. No societal evolution that brings life in nations was built on relativism. When we govern with the mindset that truth has different versions, and there are no absolutes, evil or good, it becomes whatever is relative at the moment we move towards the undoing of any nation. Then, we begin to question all absolutes. Our Republic was founded on the premise that there is a God, and He is involved in the matters of nations and He has given unalienable rights to the people. At the birth of our nation, we placed our trust in the Word of God as His written manual to establish a government and lead a nation that could stand the test of time. The Declaration of Independence and Constitution are replete with the Creator's fingerprints.

The Kingdom's ecosystem, not religion, must be reestablished as the overarching belief system in our nation. Religion minimalizes our beliefs and causes us to separate from each other. The first thing we have to do as a Holy Nation within our nation, as believers, is destroy any religious thoughts or ideals that separate us from restoring our nation to what God intended.

The Word of God says that we are a holy nation, a royal priesthood, and all of us are called into it. If we do not engage in our nation now, we will suffer the fate of Edmund Burke's quote, **"The fate of good men who refuse to become involved in politics is to be ruled by evil men."** And "The greatest mistake is to do nothing because you can only do little." At the end of the day, if we fall into either one of these categories, the rules will be set up against us, evil men will rule us, and we will ultimately become slaves to the one-world system. In my opinion, we have become marginalized and minimalized now in many ways.

1. Destroy Forms

So, what do we do? **Number one**: We must begin to destroy forms. In Mark 7:13, Jesus challenged the Pharisees, who were the leading religious group of the day, the high priests of the nation. He said, "Your forms, ways, and your traditions have made the Word of God of no effect." Basically, they twisted the Word of God to fit their ways, but it separated them from God's best. We must remove any forms of religion that separate us from each other, no matter what they are. We must focus on the greater cause before us: reestablishing the ecosystem of the Kingdom and the Father's thought over our nation. There are bigger fish to fry. We must destroy ways (something in which your particular denomination believes) that separate us—for example, a certain way of worship, preaching, or dressing, etc. We must create a coalition of righteous people who will storm the gates of defilement built over our nation's psyche. Through people, the spirit of darkness has set up thrones to rule over us because we've removed ourselves from the governing process. If we don't do this, we will no longer have the freedom to fight, and we're on the verge of that now.

2. False Humility

Number two: I want to talk about false humility. Do you realize that Jesus himself became us so that we would become Him? Paul talks about this in his writings. *"He that knew no sin became sin,"* (Second Corinthians 5-21). He became sin. Jesus did not just take on your sin, but he became sin itself so that it would be destroyed on the cross. Through the death, burial, and resurrection of the Lord Jesus Christ, and His rising, we have an advocate with the Father to be one with the Father continually. Jesus prayed this in John 17:22 that as He and the Father were one, so we would be one with them. One with the Father puts you in the God-class of beings. Developing a false humility about who we are and pouring dirt on our heads, stripping our clothes, fasting, and crawling over glass to prove who we are to the Father is ridiculous. It's false humility, which is of the devil; it's not of God. This lack of understanding who we are and our identity in Him has caused us not to stand up as champions and fight for our nation.

We must remove any mindset that separates us from the political realm because of our faith in everyday life. I don't care what you think about politics, religion, or education. We have walked away and washed our hands of it in the public arena of debate and decided the world can do a better job. Our Founding Fathers would not recognize this type of Christianity in our nation today or the people who profess a belief in it. They fought for their faith and were willing to die for the chance to birth the greatest nation on earth. Does that sound like anything you hear in sermons today across our nation? We have left the room and the national debate because, just like the religious leaders in Jesus' day, we are more concerned about our comfort and not rocking the boat as long as life is working for us.

Our silence from the pulpits to the streets is deafening and has brought us to a place of great peril. "*Silence in the face of evil is itself evil: God will not hold us guiltless. Not to speak is to speak. Not to act is to act.*" (Dietrich Bonhoeffer) Let's shake off our compliancy and be the righteous voices and actions that transform our nation. We must rise again in our nation with answers from the Creator Himself in the affairs of men or suffer the plight of being enslaved by the system we have allowed to rule over us. We've allowed wolves in sheep's clothing to convince us that they're the best choice to rule over our nation. We've washed our hands of all major spheres of influence in society. We should be stepping into the top of these places and allowing the ecosystem of the Father and the Kingdom to manifest and be the overarching spirit over those areas, especially politics.

Let's remove the mindset that we need to separate faith and politics or, for that matter, any of the other spheres as well.

3. Re-establish Our Identity

Number three: We must re-establish our identity. We are now sons and daughters of God. Through Jesus' death, burial, and resurrection, He invited us into the family, making us one with the Father and Him. Interestingly, every time Jesus brought up the subject of oneness with the Father, the Pharisees wanted to kill Him. Why? In the Jewish culture, when a son grows to a certain age, the family celebrates with a party, and the son is given a ring and a robe that represents their family crest and its authority. Wherever he went, the ring would identify him. When he stamped something, it was the same as his father stamping it. When he spoke up for something, the father spoke up for it. When he did something, the father had to honor it. Likewise, when Jesus reminded others that He was one with the Father, the Pharisees wanted to kill him. (John 10-30-31)

We don't fully understand what being one with the Father means and the power it carries. When you're one with the Father, you're in His stead; you're in His authority. The Word of God says, *"Whatever you bound on Earth will be bound in Heaven. Whatever you loose on Earth, will be loosed in Heaven."* I don't think we understand who we are, so we must re-establish our identity as sons and daughters of the King. It's important we know that we are royalty set in the seat with Jesus and the Father both because we're one with Him. Jesus prayed for this, and it happened in the finished work of Jesus. He re-established you as Him because He became you that you could become Him and operate in His stead while He's gone. This is simple theology, but I know very few people who think like this at a deep level and understand we have been translated into the God class once we are born again; restored by the finished work of Jesus Himself. Let us begin to operate with the Father's ring and robe, which was provided to us in the finished work of Jesus so that we can walk in the authority given to us. He plans on us ruling with Him in this life as well as the one to come.

Time-Tested Societal Government

Number four: We must push for a time-tested societal government. All societies that do not honor absolutes fail. Relativism doesn't succeed in any generation. It might work for a few, but a country that lacks moral clarity and does not have absolutes will be destroyed from within. As Edmund Burke declared, **"There is but one law for all, namely that law which governs all laws, the law of the Creator, the law of nature and of nations."** This is the way that God governs. He is in control of all nations and the world, but He's not in charge. If He were in charge, there would be no sin, and everything would be perfect. But also, there would be no free will. Although He is in control of the universe, He left us in charge. In Genesis 1:28, we read, *"Then God blessed them, and God said to them, be fruitful and multiply; fill the earth and subdue it; have dominion over the fish of sea, and the birds in the air, and over every living thing that moves on the earth."* Also, we see in Psalms 115:16, *"The heaven, even the heavens, are the Lord's; But the earth He has given to the children of men."*

We must develop strategies and tactics. We have to create media platforms, blogs, and websites that beat with the heart of the Father in them. We each need to become people who love the community, love the neighborhood, the restorers of the breached, and rescuers of those in darkness. Through influence, trust, favor, and answers, we can interact with people instead of making our lives different because we disagree. Start building a coalition of righteous people on the earth who support the cause of establishing America upon absolute foundational truths from the Word of God. Those people are out there, trust me. Many more people in our nation believe in God, Family, and Country than don't. Proverbs 29:2 says, *"When the righteous are in*

authority, people rejoice: but when the wicked rule, the people mourn."
We must make the debate about re-establishing the right standards of
our nation again, and not only about what we believe in our particular
church or what our political persuasions are alone. What if we start
around the ideals of our founding to build a coalition of people who
believe in America's greatness and the Creator's hand in its birth using
words that have an eternal basis: wisdom, integrity, honor, discretion,
instruction, correction, discipline, prudence? Using these words as a
foundation, we can build a coalition of righteous people who will take
back what's been taken from us.

Removing religious beliefs that are not God is paramount. He said
that by observing His law and His Word, you would be the head, not
the tail. You would be above all nations of the Earth. You would be
blessed at everything you put your hand to. You would create wealth
for yourself, and the blessings of the Lord would overtake you and
your generations. The people of the Earth would know that the Lord
is your God, and they would fear you. They would revere and respect
your authority in the way God does things on Earth; the fear of the Lord
is the beginning of the Wisdom of God's way of governing nations.

These are God's provisions for His sons and daughters. Any forms,
ways, doctrines of men, false humility, and theology that does not
represent the Father's best violates these provisions. Obeying His
Word takes precedence and creates the foundation for everything else.
There has to be a council of the whole will of God when rules are
implemented for governing our nation. We cannot lead without wealth
or respect. We cannot invade, go to the top of spheres of influence,
and favor without being the head and not the tail. False humility and
the ways and structures that men have given us have caused us to separate from society and not embrace the mandate to disciple nations.
We have to train new champions who believe the Word and its
description of who they are to save our nation.

We must restore our broken foundation and develop unity in the body of Christ and all who believe in America. Unity doesn't mean we all agree on everything. But what are some things that we can agree on that help to define this group of believers? They believe in

- The moral fabric of our country
- Absolutes
- Law and order
- Governing from foundational laws that are unchangeable
- You cannot govern as a society if you go down the path on which anything is accepted, and relativism becomes the law of the day

We need to build a coalition to usher in new Founding Fathers and Mothers, and ideas and thoughts that are applicable to the 21st century that people will want to hear.

The 80/20 rule applies here. If I believe in 80% of what you believe in as far as righteousness and the Word of God is concerned, we ought to be able to walk together. We might not fellowship every day, go to ballgames, or go to church together. The point is the Coalition of Righteous people must come together in a movement to take our country back from the evil and darkness that has invaded our land. It's a bigger cause than our individual lives at this point. The great champion David said, "Isn't there not a cause? Why are we not doing something?" As 14 or 15-year-old kid, David went to the front lines of battle. He looked at grown soldiers and asked, "Why isn't somebody doing something? Is there not a cause?"

It's time to take our country back. If we don't do this now, when will we do it? If we don't do this now when will be the right time? When we're in chains and have to suffer as martyrs? Is that it will take to get your attention? The religious leaders of Hitler's day allowed him to do everything he did and, by and large, stayed silent until they became martyrs. By then, it was too late! Is that what we're going to do? I hope not. I'm in this thing for the long haul for my children and my children's children.

Let us embrace God's plan for generations. Think about how our great, great, great, great-grandchildren will fare because we lived. Emerson is quoted as saying, "Success in life for me now is when I leave that all the people closest to me, they would have breathed a little bit easier because I existed." We should rule and govern this way in America as believers. What will you do with the freedom you have? Let us rise up as a Holy Nation within our nation and do what's right in the Father's eyes.

Chapter 8

New Founding Fathers and Mothers: Knights Rising

In this chapter, we will discuss strategies to infiltrate the world the way Jesus taught His disciples. In Matthew 13:24-33, we see three different parables about how the Kingdom works in the world.

- **First,** He talks about sowing seed in a field and the enemy coming in at night and sowing tares.

- **Second,** we see that when sown, the mustard seed becomes the largest tree of herbs.

- **Third,** He explains that only a small amount of leaven is needed to leaven the whole lump. I want to break these three strategies down, look at what they have in common and what Jesus is attempting to get us to understand out of them.

Number one: Each of these acts essentially goes unnoticed; the ground doesn't know what kind of seed is put in until the plant or tree springs up. When the seed and the leaven are put into the ground and the dough, they go into darkness where no one can see what's being produced until it's too late.

Number two: Jesus states that when He returns, it will be like a thief in the night; no one will be expecting it. Second Thessalonians 5:2 states, *"For yourselves know perfectly that the day of the Lord cometh as a thief in the night."* We see that the enemy in the first story came at night when no one could see him, like a thief in the night. All three parables indicate that the Kingdom comes in unnoticed by that in which it's sown into or placed. The ground and the dough have no idea what they are getting ready to birth.

Number three: When the soil cracks open and the plant bursts forth, it is too late. The soil cannot retract what it grew, and the dough can't go back to its original size before the leaven hidden in it expands. Jesus states in Luke 16:7, *"That the sons of darkness are wiser in their generation than the sons of light."* In Matthew 10:16, Jesus tells His disciples to, *"be wise as serpents and harmless as doves."* As we explore how to be light in the world and have answers the world is looking for, let's look at how Jesus Himself taught us to invade the world system through the wisdom from the Father, which will have the power to save not only our nation but others as well. The conclusion of how to invade the world system is pretty simple. Be wise as serpents and study how the sons of darkness implement their plans. Finally, go into every sphere with the people and the systems being unaware of who you are because, through the wisdom of the Father, you will bring answers they have been unable to access. You might look like them on the outside, but the Kingdom is hidden inside you. Remember, be wise as serpents. We can carry and place the leaven and seeds of the Kingdom as He directs in the people, systems, and our nation, watching them grow and overtake the darkness until there's nothing but light. Let's begin!

To change our current system, we must invade the world as Knights Rising. The rising part in us is the leaven of the Kingdom. As we begin to release it and hide it in the people He is sending us to, we will start to see "His Kingdom come, His will be done on Earth as it is in Heaven" to change the very things He has on His heart for our nation and people in it. We must be wise as serpents for the knights to invade the world's systems that have been turned against us in America. The tables have been turned completely in favor of the wrong spirit that seeks to destroy our nation.

In 2018, The Lord showed me in a dream two numbers: 1908 and 2008. I believe these numbers represent the last century and, in fact, when this great shift began to happen in our nation. At its roots was a plan of darkness to take over our institutions of higher education. It would then filter into every level of our educational systems from grade school through universities, sowing and propagating their seeds and world views to rewrite history in the hearts of the youth. Then through a well-crafted plan of revision, they would brainwash one generation, beginning the great unraveling that would ultimately destroy our nation. If they could get the education sphere, they would eventually control all others because children would be indoctrinated with what they taught. Does this thought sound hauntingly familiar, like a thief coming in the night to sow tares among the wheat or someone coming in to put a little leaven in the lump? To remind you of what Edmund Burke said, "You see all it takes for evil to triumph is for good men and women of conscience to do nothing." When we weren't looking, the antichrist came in, clothed in sheep's clothing, and through the very tools the Creator gave us to rule with, it has almost destroyed our great nation. "Education is the cheap defense of nations," Burke said. If the righteous people lose charge of our education system, we will eventually lose our nation as we've known it.

Lenin stated, "Give me one generation of youth in America, and I will destroy her from within." We are there. Between the years 1908 and 2008, the two numbers I saw in my dream, the tables have turned. The very people, the very societal values and foundation of the Kingdom of God on which our country was founded, what we believed in at one time, have come under attack and nearly eliminated from public debate in our country. Over the last hundred years, we as believers have all but abandoned the spheres and influences that disciple a nation. We are now experiencing what Lenin prophesied.

The time has come to go in as Knights, unnoticed, as we move with Kingdom wisdom and insights that the Father gives. Then we will begin to restore our individual spheres, and only then will we be called to save our nation collectively. We have to slip in the side door unnoticed to ascend the places of influence that we are called to and begin to drop leaven and plant wheat among tares. We have to reverse the curse sown by the enemy and operate out of the spirit of what Jesus taught and place the seeds of wheat for tares and leaven for the unleavened parts, beginning the restoration process. This is not about imposing our will upon the whole nation; this is about releasing our influence and showing them the answers on how wonderful the Father is, so they'll have a choice.

The Father is releasing His wisdom in us so that we can ascend the spheres of influence and rise to the top. Our goal should be to free the systems in the atmosphere above those places so that people have a choice to see the Father. As long as people are bound by darkness and the enemy's deception in the atmosphere and flooded by delusion because of the spirit of darkness that's there, they can't see well enough to make a choice. Paul addresses this in Ephesians 6:10-18, stating, *"We don't wrestle against flesh and blood but against spiritual wickedness in heavenly places. We must start to rise and pull-down principalities, powers, and might which come against God's design for our nation."* In 2 Corinthians 4:4, we read, *"In whom the God of this world hath blinded the minds of them which believe not, lest the light of the glorious gospel of Christ, who is the image of God, should shine unto them."* Unless we contest for our cities by removing darkness, people are held and blinded by it.

To begin this process, we have to reinvigorate believers. We need to create platforms that can lead to movements and facilitate what the Father is birthing right now in our nation. They are out there, those who see our plight and are ready to step in at this time in history. The Lord showed me this group of people who will not bend, they won't bow, and they won't back down from this heavenly call and destiny. They will be **Spiritual Wrecking Balls** to any and all altars of Baal that we have allowed to be built, especially in the arenas of church and politics. Take time to read what this group will look like in Joel 2:1-12. They will become the catalyst of our day and move through the land, setting people free and destroying darkness. By this, they will restore the nation to its roots and foundation of the Creator. We must begin invigorating the cause of freedom for the nation at once.

What is the clarion call? To disciple nations. It hasn't changed. We need to start in America and as we gain success, extend it to other nations. We have to find and invigorate this vision by discipling people who will give everything to be the Knights who rise. I'm often asked, "How will you take on a task so large and find the people who will be in the game for the long haul?" It is very simple, but it won't necessarily be easy. The people will find you and me when we Blow the Trumpet in Zion **(Be The Catalyst).** At the beginning of this verse, the Lord revealed to me that it implies you and I should be the catalyst in our sphere of influence, and as we do, it would attract the people He is calling to it.

So, that's what I am doing and encouraging others to do. The Lord used Edmund Burke's quote to inspire me to write two books that would be a part of the movement He is starting. "He that does nothing because he can only do little has made no greater mistake." You are reading what began as the little I could do. Let's look at Gideon's story, which might help clarify how one person can bring change to a nation. In the book of Judges, starting in Chapter 6, Gideon is trying to survive in a nation that has been taken over by God's enemy. He has an encounter with the angel of the Lord while he is hiding, trying to get enough food to eat and live. Although the Lord tells him, "I am with you to save your nation," Gideon comes up with many excuses of why he can't (like we do). After many signs from God, he finally accepts the call to save his people. He gathered 30,000 people to help fight, still way less than the enemy they faced. Then the Lord took Gideon and his troops through several tests to see who would qualify to go to war. In the end, only 300 people were left! Think about it! Weren't you just thinking that saving our nation might be too big a task? How about 300 men saving the nation of Israel? When Gideon's army started winning battles throughout the towns, he gained more warriors with each win. By the time they reached the last town, the whole nation had joined the movement that the Lord began with just Gideon. A man God found hiding, trying to survive, and he saved an entire nation!

We have to determine in our hearts that we will find and disciple those who are ready now. We must envision how we can go into our nation's systems and develop at least a 50-year plan to invade, advance, and increase the Kingdom of God in every sphere. In Isaiah 54:2, the text reads, *"Enlarge the place of your tent and let them stretch forth the curtains of your habitations: spare not, lengthen thy cords, and strengthen thy stakes."* When we enlarge in us what's possible and dream about the things we want to see in our nation, we will have the strength to go up the spheres as knights. We will gain momentum and people who hear the sound of reformation. The world around us will join us because of the answers and vision for the country that we bring. They will see the light, seeing something different on you. As they join, they will help stretch forth the cords of the Kingdom. We will find people who will be champions for a just cause. They'll see it even though they might be in the world. God will begin to open their eyes because He knows they can be part of the movement to stretch forth the cords of His habitation. Then we will be able to go further than we thought. God knows the people who are ready, and we need all of them to come and join His cause.

As you overcome and the Father gives you victory at every level just like He did to Gideon, you will find people who will go with you. The Lord has shown me that we haven't had His influence at the top of the spheres and systems because we haven't mobilized and started to ascend. This has been our problem. We keep standing at the bottom, praying for Him to do something. He's thinking, "I gave you the keys to the Kingdom. I put you in charge and left. What don't you understand about that? You need to go up the mountain, and as you go, I'll be with you." Notice He was *with* Gideon. He was *with* Joshua. He was *with* David. He was *with* Abraham. He didn't do it *for* them. He went *with* them. He isn't going to do our part, but He will go with us. We have developed a faulty theology, always waiting for Him to do it for us. We tend to be like Elijah, who would have spent the rest of his life in a cave had God not challenged him to think differently and believe that He would be with him as he went.

We think we are alone when God has something big that He wants to accomplish, like saving a nation. However, He always has hidden resources when we decide step in. He said to Elijah, "There are 7000 others like you just as powerful! They just don't have national prominence." They didn't bow their knees to Jezebel. I'm sure that statement took Elijah by surprise because he thought he was the only one left. The reality is there were 7000 other champions in Israel. Back then, Israel was a small place; it's hard for me to believe he didn't know any of these 7000 people. He'd gotten so messed up in his mind that he either forgot they were alive, or he bought into the lie (like us) that all hope is lost for our nation. I believe they were a people ready for the battle, champions waiting for him to blow the trumpet. Be the catalyst they need to see step in now. Who is waiting on you right now to show up in your powerful state, that they might hear the sound of your trumpet and join the march to restore Old Glory?

We should create media platforms, write books, start a blog, or do a podcast to find each other and initiate the movement the Father wants to unleash. We have to become facilitators of righteousness and follow His plan to take back our nation. We have to facilitate what the Father is doing. The Father is trying His best in this season to show His sons and daughters how powerful they are. "Are you going to rise as Knights? Are you going to find your true identity and start acting like sons and daughters instead of playing the role of an orphan? Are you going to do it?" We have to become facilitators of influence and answers and thereby winning favor with people.

We must construct new foundations, new thoughts, and new thought leaders. It's not about making Christianity edgy; it's about making the King be seen. Trust me; if people see Jesus and the Father on you, they will want Him. The tree of life seen lived through us, where the Father shows up through His sons and daughters. This is where people will begin to taste and see that the Lord is good through His children. Paul said, "We are epistles read and learned of all men." We are His epistles read and learned of all men. So, how do they really learn? Not by just talking, but by presence, power, love, influence, favor, and answers. That is why everyone was attracted to Jesus. Everywhere He went, people were drawn to Him. He had to go to the mountain to hide from people. No one hated Him except the Pharisees and Romans, who were a very small percentage of the population. Wherever Jesus went, everyone in Jerusalem liked him. Why? When they saw Him, they saw the Father. They could see the Father's love, power, acceptance, influence, and answers.

We currently don't lead in any of the spheres of influence in our world; we must change that now or suffer the consequences of being a slave to the world systems under the direct control of darkness. We must start to measure success in the church again by Jesus's primary measurement, which is the discipleship of nations, as stated in Matthew 28:18-20. We have more churches in America than ever before. However, we have lost most of our national influence to shape culture in any spheres of influence. We must begin to major in the major things of the Kingdom of God and minor in the minor things if we want this to change. If not, we will suffer a life of servitude to the spirit of this world which has taken charge in the absence of *the giant slayers and champions of the King, you and me.*

Chapter 9

The Secret Weapon – YOU

This chapter is appropriately titled "The Secret Weapon – YOU" because I want you to begin seeing the greatness the Father put in you. All you need to do is dig out the treasure already there as He highlights it. You *are* the secret weapon and have answers for the people around you that will change the world. In Psalms 139:14, we read, *"You are fearfully and wonderfully made."* He continues that you were made in secret and skillfully put together. In other words, there were skillsets and abilities in you before you were formed in your mother's womb. There were secret things put inside of you that only the Creator could see. He put them there on purpose, for a great destiny that He wants to walk out with you as His sons and daughters. In Ruth 2:16, Boaz *"told his servants to let fall the handfuls of purpose for her and leave them that she might glean them or find them."*

It's interesting that the secret weapon is within you, in your make-up and DNA from the Father, hidden from everyone, even you. There are also handfuls of purpose planted out in the future that you know nothing about yet. In Psalms 139:16b, the text reads, *"The days were fashioned for me, when as yet there were none of them."* That's right! Purpose, dreams, and destiny that you haven't even discovered yet exist for you.

One of the great insights I received 14 years ago was that **He doesn't hide things *from* me; He hides things *for* me** and reveals them when it's time. Remember when you hid Easter eggs for your kids? When they are three or four years old, you put them out in plain sight. But, when they're eight or ten, you have to hide them really well. Their age determined how you would hide the eggs. I think the Father is the same way. As a matter of fact, I know He is. I've lived enough life to have some handfuls of purpose suddenly appear when I was ready, and the timing was right. Some of it was about me being ready, but some of it was about the timing. He's the only one who knows the timing **(Father knows best).** As I have walked out my life, I have run into some of these handfuls of purpose and secrets hidden inside of me that I didn't know existed before then.

There are times in your life when the handfuls of purpose show up, and it's time to manifest them and step into the new level of life that's revealed. It's about you are growing into mature sons and daughters, but it's also about the Father's timing. Even when we don't understand. we must always remember that Father knows best, and His timing is always perfect.

In the previous chapter, we talked about how you have to keep growing into who you are because the Secret is you and in you. Peter talks about us being multifaceted and multilayered, or multicolored in 1 Peter 4:10, *"As each one has received a gift, minister it to one another as good stewards of the manifold grace of God."* The word manifold means multilayered grace. You were born with layers of answers for the world around you, and the grace to discover them is unlimited because it comes from Him. Then Paul talks about being members in particular and that each joint supplies. In 1 Corinthians 12:21, he says, *"The hand cannot sayeth to the foot 'I don't have need of you.'"* You are in the body, so you have many layers, manifold grace, empowerment, and secrets inside you. These layers can be compared to secret weapons the Father is waiting to release at the right time and season to enforce the destruction that Jesus has already rendered to darkness and pull it down in His name. He has made you with powerful answers for the world He is calling you to explore; we must begin to take this seriously and GO!

Our greatest issue is a lack of action due to a neutered belief in who we are and who our Father is, which keeps us from ascending our individual spheres. He began to reveal this to me almost four years ago now. We haven't been going up because we don't think that we'll make a difference if we do.

I have mentioned the following before, but it's worth repeating. **Number one:** The greatest sin is to do nothing because you can only do little.

Number two: If you decide not to be involved in politics and the governing of our society, you are choosing to be ruled by evil men. Our Founding Fathers understood this, but we've lost sight of it. Jesus understood this, as we see in Luke 16:10, *"If you're not faithful in little, why would the master make you ruler of much?"* It's the same thing that Edmund Burke said, "The greatest mistake is doing nothing because you can only do little." It sounds similar to me, and that's probably where he got it from.

Your identity and the secret things coming out of you are the answer to the world's problems. You won't have the solutions to every problem, but you will have the solutions to some. The secret is in you, in part. As you ascend the spheres that you're called to, the answers will be revealed. We're concerned we won't have the answers as we go, but the only way you'll get the answers is to go. In Proverbs 16:1, we see, *"The preparations of the heart belong to man, but the answer of the tongue is from the Lord."* Then in Proverbs 16:9, *"A man's heart plans his way, but the Lord directs his steps."* I believe we haven't received direction because we aren't doing our part by planning! We keep waiting for the answers and directions, but we are not doing our part first. We keep waiting for Him to do or show us something, but it is on us to prepare our hearts and make plans to our best ability, and then He will do His thing. The Father's timing is perfect, but He won't step in and do our part or allow it to dwarf our growth process of becoming champions so that He can reveal another layer of our destiny. He will keep things hidden even in us and for us until the time is right. When revealed, it will have potential answers that can save whole nations.

Let's look at some examples of the Father preparing people and then uncovering them in His timing. Joseph was hidden in a prison of all places. Esther was in the very courts of the king, hidden in plain sight. Moses was placed in the river Nile to save his life until it was time for the deliverer to show up. They were all hidden. Think about Ruth, who came from a nation in which she lost her husband. Naomi, Ruth's mother-in-law, lost her husband and son. They had no men. At that time, if you didn't have a man, you were in trouble. They went back to their homeland, and somehow Ruth ended up in the fields of Boaz trying to survive. Boaz, part of Jesus's lineage, took Ruth in; they fell in love and married. Ruth became part of the lineage of Jesus, yet she had no idea she had become part of the story that would ultimately bring forth the Savior of the world. Talk about impact!

In her handfuls of purpose, Ruth helped birth someone who wouldn't save only a nation but the whole world! She was just a woman caught up in a bad situation, with no idea she had such a great purpose and potential. How about you? What greatness is in you right now, crying out to be released? If Ruth could step into her story, can't you? Don't you believe you were made for something more? You must begin to believe in your greatness, so we can unseat the darkness attempting to destroy America.

We are His authoritative enforcement agency on earth, left here by the King himself. He gave us the keys and said, "You take care of it." If we don't enforce His finished work upon the enemy, the enemy will thrive and maintain His access and power in the atmosphere. If we enforced the total destruction that Jesus has already rendered, He would be bound because that's what the Word of God says. *"Whatever you bind, I will bind."* If we bind Him, He can't have the access that He would like. If we don't, He will rule over us. This is what has happened.

If we have answers by Word of the Father, when we ascend our spheres, those answers will neuter the enemy's policies that he is attempting to propagate and grow. Deception and delusion happen to people who can't see. Delusion is the first step toward a deception in which you can see partly. Deception is when you're completely under the water. As you ascend the places, He's calling to you with superior answers, and when the others around you realize it, you can clean up the atmosphere and bring fresh sight to those affected by the delusion. As you go, and the answers are revealed in their time, the delusion will be broken over some people, and they will turn and follow you in the cause that's in you. They will have a change of heart and go with you. The strength that comes from them going with you will help get you to the next level. We must go up and be willing to fight in the spirit and pull these things down and release the answers. If you release the answers from the Father, it will break the power of darkness because it's already being defeated. We must make the enemy and his thoughts inadequate because they are.

We have to show up with the Wisdom from another world to show that the enemy's answers are incomplete. We have to jam the answer into the realm of the spirit and break the power of that thing so that the deluded ones will see. Some of the deceived ones will break free through the realization that they've bought into an incomplete truth, which is a lie propagated by the enemy. This is not about people, but about principalities and us ascending and letting the Father keep us hidden until it's time to destroy the yoke of the enemy with His power.

We must begin to reveal the enemy's plans through the truth. The incomplete and twisted truths are indeed insufficient for the world's problems. Our answers should cause a realization to come to others that they had not yet considered. For example, on many occasions, I believed the answers I was applying in my business were not only the right ones but were the best and on the cutting edge of our industry at that time. Suddenly, I would see or read something that would challenge the current belief and premise I was living under and thought was wonderful. At that moment, I was introduced to a superior way of doing things, making the old ways seem obsolete.

To summarize, the Secret is *you*. You are the Father's secret weapon being prepared for battle. We must insert our truth into the atmosphere as we climb, just like leaven being placed into the dough. We jam the truth of who God is into the atmosphere, and like jamming a frequency in nature, we jam the frequency of the enemy through the finished work of Jesus, enforcing the enemy's destruction that Jesus already won. This battle is not against people but spiritual wickedness in high places. When you break the power over the minds of people, they can see with freed sight, and have the complete truth rendered to them. Then they have a choice, and I believe most people will choose the superior from the Father if we give it to them.

Chapter 10

You Were a Caterpillar,
and Now You Are a Butterfly

The metamorphosis of a caterpillar to a butterfly is the Kingdom story of intrigue and insertion of the Kingdom's leaven in us as a people able to carry His very presence and glory into our realm of influence. As His Kingdom gets into people and systems, they take on the Father's original intent. Paul gives us insight into this metamorphosis in 2 Corinthians 4:18, *"But we all, with unveiled face, beholding as in a mirror the glory of the Lord, are being transformed into the same from glory to glory just as by the Spirit of the Lord."* This is incredible when you consider we are infused with God's glory. It is like looking into a mirror at our natural face; we are changed into the same image as Him. What if by the power of transformation of the Holy Spirit we carry the King and the Kingdom into the world? Can we reverse the curse by going into the tares as a thief in the night like Jesus? That's the way the Master is coming. What if we represent Him in this way and sow wheat among tares? By taking the seedtime and harvest tools the Creator set into motion, we sow the Kingdom into the systems and people, and then a metamorphosis takes place in them. Suddenly, the Kingdom explodes in and through them.

No matter what type of turf you have, a healthy lawn is the best defense against weeds or tares. It is difficult for them to grow among strong roots competing for the same moisture and nutrients as the thriving turf. If you create the ecosystem around it and keep feeding that turf, tares (weeds) have a hard time growing. The healthy root system allows you to easily get rid of weeds that appear. This is one of the keys to the Kingdom. We must go in unnoticed, or undercover if you will, bringing solutions that were not previously accessible.

These answers to problems in their lives will cause them to rethink what they believe about you. When people gain access to the Father's answers for them, their perception about Him and you is the first thing that really changes in them. Why? Because you just showed up with something they couldn't access. It's awesome when this happens because you immediately have their attention and favor.

This happened to me the other day. I was having a conversation with my friend Stephen. I was struggling with a few of my own issues, but I couldn't get them resolved for some reason. Although he was not trying to fix me or give me the answers, he asked me two questions that completely interrupted my pattern and caused me to re-evaluate my thoughts and actions. I realized that what he was sharing had the breath of God on it, and it changed my heart immediately. By the next morning, I was completely free from that pattern of thought, thereby taking a new set of actions.

How did that happen? He had superior answers inside of him. He didn't realize he was releasing them to me for the questions I needed answers to, but there was power in his words. This is how transform-ation, metamorphosis, and conversion happen. You *were* a caterpillar; you *are* a butterfly. When you make the transition from darkness to light, you *were* darkness; now you *are* light. It's a conversion exper-ience, which is at the essence and the core of metamorphosis. As we go into the systems of thought, having superior answers and/or questions that will stimulate the conversation in the direction that the Father wants to release something, then a transformation occurs naturally.

You were a caterpillar, and now you are a butterfly because you were transformed. Transformation automatically happens everywhere His fingertips and His fingers are inside you. His hands are your hands now. His feet are your feet now. You are His authority on planet earth, whether you believe it or not. He has released the keys of the Kingdom to us so we can go into the systems to put leaven in them and sow wheat. The goal is to bring people into ultimate transformation and give them the best that the Father has for them.

When people see the Father, Jesus, or the Holy Spirit, and they have been set free because the atmosphere is filled with the Father's thoughts about them, and they will want Him. Nobody who truly sees the Father will turn away because He is just that wonderful!

People are not converted for several reasons. Number one, they never see the real Father. Jesus came saying, *"I come for one reason, to do the will of Him who sent me. I come so you might know the Father."* The emphasis here is on the fact that all the people that day didn't know the Father. He was inferring that you've never met the Father; the entire Jewish race had never met the Father!

Jesus is the perfect blueprint of who the Father is, was, and will always be. He is the prototype. He is the Son, the Christ, and the Messiah. He lived a perfect life that showed people who the Father was. He said, "If you've seen me, you've seen the Father." Notice the emphasis. People won't see how good He is and recognize they want to be with Him if the enemy blinds them. People won't enter the Kingdom if they don't believe what they're seeing is true. The devil has deceived them, and the enemy blinds their minds. We must enforce the destruction that Jesus has already rendered on the enemy.

The enemy doesn't have any power; he was stripped of it. The Word of God says in Colossians 2:15, *"He was disarmed, and annihilated and completely put under."* There wasn't anything left. Jesus took the keys that Adam had given to him, and He gave them to us. The keys that Jesus is talking about were the ones originally given to Adam to take dominion and subdue and be fruitful upon the face of the earth. Adam and Eve willingly gave them to the enemy because of deception. When the last Adam, Jesus, died, was buried, and then resurrected, He went into hell and took the keys the devil had stolen through deception and said, *"I'll take those back. All authority in Heaven and earth has been given to me."* He's the King. He said, *"All authority has been given. Now, I give it to you, go and disciple the nations."*

The keys of the Kingdom are the keys to take dominion over the earth, subdue it, and be fruitful and multiply. What do we make fruitful and multiply? The Father's will, the Father's intentions, the Father's transformation, and the Father's heart for people. This is not a war against flesh; this is a war against principalities and darkness in high places that have deceived people. The devil can only use the systems that were set up previously. When he gets ahold of them, he corrupts them. If you notice in Ezekiel 28, it says that the devil was corrupted. The corruption came out of the transgression. When the devil gets ahold of the systems that God set up to benefit us, he corrupts them and makes them dark instead of light. That's all he has; he has no light. He is darkness.

As we learn how to walk with the Father going up our spheres, we have an opportunity to watch others experience a metamorphosis. We have the Father's fingerprints inside of us, so what we touch, He touches. We bring transformation to those atmospheres that we're in. We break the power of darkness over people, giving them the chance to have a conversion, a rebirth experience. The complete description of what our metamorphosis looks like is being born again. You are now a new creature in Christ. Old things are passed away, behold all things are new. This is what happens to people when they truly see the light of the Father.

I have a hard time believing that anyone who has truly seen the Lord wouldn't want Him because He's so beautiful. He's the lily of the valley. He's the fairest among ten thousand. He's the desire of all nations. Rebirth happens when you run into something bigger than we are, then let go of the darkness and receive the light. This is the essence of conversion.

Reformation

Lastly, let's look at reform. Reformation only comes through transformation, which comes by metamorphosis. Metamorphosis and transformation are the same, equal and interchangeable. When those things happen, rebirth happens. When you're transformed, or you have a metamorphosis, you are converted. You are a new creature. If you walk it out properly as He intended, you begin to disciple nations with this experience.

In John 3:16-17, we read, *"That God so loved the world that He gave His only begotten Son, that whoever believes in Him should not perish but have everlasting life. For God did not send His Son into the world to condemn the world, but that the world through Him might be saved."* God mentions the world systems four times and man once. The emphasis is four to one; the word for world there is described as cosmos or systems or an orderly arrangement. There are orderly arrangements in the atmosphere of doing life here that God set up to benefit us. If the devil gets control of them, he turns them into darkness, and the very thing that was meant for our good, the devil turns to evil. According to Edmund Burke, if good men refuse to become involved in each sphere, especially politics, evil men, will rule over you.

This is what we're experiencing now. I've been taught all my life not to talk about politics and religion because you're just going to get into arguments with others, and it's not worth it. However, we need to start a dialogue from the Kingdom perspective now because if we don't, we will be ruled over by evil men. We are already under darkness in our nation at varying degrees. We have to go in the systems with something superior that releases that atmosphere of the Kingdom upon people and the systems and save the systems of the world. You could say, *"The Father so loved the world that He gave His only begotten Son that whosoever believeth Him would be saved."* The systems themselves, which were set up for our benefit, were organically endued with the power and the seed of the Father being able to reproduce itself in like kind. When they're taken over by the enemy, which is the keys, the enemy turns them into dark portals that control the spheres.

We've haven't had reformation in my lifetime in these spheres because reformation means you've reformed from the top down. Then, you have a renaissance and a great awakening, which will sweep through our great nation in every arena of life. That's what we must go after, that's the target. If we don't go, who will?

If He doesn't send us, who will go? I'm going. I hope you will, too, and we create a movement that renews the systems with the Father's DNA again. I want to see a world in which we would be proud for our great, great, great-grandchildren to grow up and know that our deposit, lives, and handfuls of purpose were on purpose for them. That's my biggest dream and goal. Let us begin to rise as the champions the Father has called each of us to be and save our nation.

Conclusion

What will happen to the United States? Will she be saved and begin a new season of her God-given destiny or fall into the trap of the ruling elites who seek to destroy her?

The answer to these questions depends on you and me. Will we begin to rise as agents of Kingdom Cultural change or fall into the trap of darkness that's attempting to hijack our nation and place it on the Titanic of Socialism, never to return to the land of the free and home of the brave?

I started my journey down the path of saving our nation with a simple question from an encounter I had with the Lord: "Will you teach my people to be more worldly?" My first response was, "This will go over like a lead balloon." Somehow, still, I knew immediately and intuitively what He was saying. I began to be open to new insights that led me to writing "The Blueprint of God: the wisdom to change the world is in YOU" and this book.

The first book in the blueprint series explored uncovering our identity and a road to personal discovery and destiny. I realized that this book had to introduce us to applying what was discovered in us for the greater purpose of fulfilling the great commission, which was to disciple nations. Through these insights, I started to see how to be *in* the world but not be *of* it. One of the most significant missing ingredients in the church today is activating *"Being wise as serpents but harmless as doves"* (Matthew 10-19) – a subject, by the way, I've never heard taught in any depth in the church my entire lifetime.

As I attempted to unpack this revelation, I understood why, and I told the Lord that no one will like being identified with the serpent. Still, as I worked through my objections in writing my first book, I started to see what He was unraveling. What if we were given the gifts that wisdom bestowed upon the serpent? Here's a few: the Seal of perfection, full of the summation of wisdom itself, perfect in beauty. Finally, the word states he was perfect in all his ways! So, what if being wise as serpents gave us access to some of these same attributes?

Hopefully, you can see the genius that the Father hid in Wisdom itself. My goal for this book is to point to the five foundational scriptures that give us a large part of the blueprint from the Son of God Himself that lays out incremental steps needed to invade every sphere, bringing heaven to earth, and changing the ecosystem over each of the seven mind molders of society. There are more than five obviously, but I believe by activating these, we can begin the very process of discipling nations.

Matthew 10-19 has the primary thought. Matthew 13-28-33 is at the end of the parable of the sower and introduces us to three insights to growing and building Kingdom influence. Finally, in Luke 16, the story of the unjust steward shows us how the world is shrewder than the sons of light, and the master comments the unjust steward in the story for, in essence, using wisdom in conducting his business affairs. These are the starting points for us to begin to gain influence once again in our nation. I realize that saving and restoring a nation is a big thought, but this is what Kingdom sons and daughters do. We are well able to save our nation because God is with us. It starts with implementing those little things we have control over in our daily lives, like leaven in the lump. If you are not faithful in little, how will you be faithful in much? *"He that does nothing because he can only do little has made no greater mistake."*

I believe we must start spreading the Kingdom within our spheres of occupation and then in our communities and cities. I can hear you asking, "Where would I start? It seems too big and overwhelming. Can we really do it?" Yes, with God, all things are possible!

I want to finish with what happened to me and how the Lord invited me to be part of this great mission He initiated. It really all started with the verse be wise as serpents and harmless as doves. That He was uncovering His ways through the Word to bring reform to our great nation and was I willing to follow Him on this journey. I decided to follow then the revelations, and insights exploded into the book you've just read. So, as I studied the things, He revealed to me, it led me on the journey to find what I could do to help restore America to the destiny the Father originally had in mind. You are reading my second book on the subject of blueprint and how if we as a people will find ours, the very DNA of God worked through us will change the world around us in a profound way.

So, my challenge to you is to find your part to play in this grand unfolding story. I hesitate to give you a list because you need to find your own path, but my publisher insisted that I throw out some things to consider doing to make a difference.

- Start a blog on something in which you burn to see change
- Find like-minded people in your community and brainstorm to come up with something you can do to win your city
- Start a business and create more wealth to fund the causes that are already making a difference in our nation
- Write a book (as you can see, this is part of what I'm doing)
- If you have a knack for it, speak at different events that align with the cause you are promoting
- Start a bible study and cover topics on subjects about transforming your community and city.
- Start a YouTube channel
- Get involved with the political process in your district
- Run for the school board
- Run for public office
- Support Godly candidates who are running for office

- Start a podcast
- Be a guest on other people's podcasts
- Find radio stations that support the nation being turned back to our Godly heritage and be a guest on their talk show
- Develop training courses based on God's destiny for America or in your field of expertise that will help facilitate His life for others.

The above is a short list of activities to consider taking on to bring His Kingdom ecosystem into your city and state. Do something and don't stay silent at this time. Find some way to place your hand and heart and go after it with all your strength. Remember, "He that does nothing because he can only do little has made no greater mistake." Obviously, I would encourage you to find something that you burn for and feel gifted in to pursue. I believe the very fire and gifting inside you are an invitation from the Father to make a difference in this life. Will America be restored to her former destiny? We are being called at this time to do our duty as His Kingdom representatives and step in to make the difference! Will we do it? I hope you will join me as one of the knights rising to take back our nation!

About Don Long

Don W. Long is a respected serial entrepreneur and founder of two businesses that have generated over $100 million in sales spanning three decades.

As a fifth-generation business owner, Don took everything he learned from his family to survive a humbling period as a door-to-door salesman selling Krispy Kreme Donuts, alarms, vacuums, 18-wheeler courses, and other products. In 1986, Don became a partner in a venture that rose to the top five percent in its industry. By 2017, one of Don's businesses ranked the top 1% of companies in the US in their industry, and in 2019, he sold that business to begin a new journey.

Don's strategic business background and his belief in embracing your true identity is an ingredient for success. He is highly sought by executive leaders, entrepreneurs, and small business owners who seek Don's message when they desire to attract more significant gains in life and business using transformational eternal principles.

Don is the author of two books, *The Blueprint of God* and the international bestselling book *Sell or Don't Eat*. Businesses and organizations across the country actively work with Don to learn how to create wealth and activate their inner greatness to excel in faith, family, finances, and business.

Don's cross-disciplinary teaching style is a match for corporate training, conferences, panels, and workshops. As an experienced entrepreneur and speaker, Don inspires audiences to seek radical transformation through his direct, relatable, and passionate speaking style. He has been married to love of his life, Cindy, for 39 years, and has two beautiful daughters, Ashton and Jordan. He currently resides in the Research Triangle area of North Carolina.

To contact Don

Email: coaching@donwlong.com

Visit his website at donwlong.com

www.ingramcontent.com/pod-product-compliance
Lightning Source LLC
Chambersburg PA
CBHW070933210326
41520CB00021B/6924